FOUR CORNERS

Second Edition

Student's Book
with Online Self-Study and Online Workbook

JACK C. RICHARDS & DAVID BOHLKE

CAMBRIDGE
UNIVERSITY PRESS

CAMBRIDGE
UNIVERSITY PRESS

University Printing House, Cambridge CB2 8BS, United Kingdom

One Liberty Plaza, 20th Floor, New York, NY 10006, USA

477 Williamstown Road, Port Melbourne, VIC 3207, Australia

314–321, 3rd Floor, Plot 3, Splendor Forum, Jasola District Centre, New Delhi – 110025, India

79 Anson Road, #06–04/06, Singapore 079906

Cambridge University Press is part of the University of Cambridge.

It furthers the University's mission by disseminating knowledge in the pursuit of education, learning and research at the highest international levels of excellence.

www.cambridge.org
Information on this title: www.cambridge.org/fourcorners

First published 2012
Second edition 2019

20 19 18 17 16 15 14 13 12 11 10 9 8 7 6 5 4 3 2 1

Printed in the United Kingdom by Latimer Trend

A catalogue record for this publication is available from the British Library

ISBN 978-1-108-55989-8 Student's Book with Online Self-Study 4
ISBN 978-1-108-55990-4 Student's Book with Online Self-Study 4A
ISBN 978-1-108-63118-1 Student's Book with Online Self-Study 4B
ISBN 978-1-108-56025-2 Student's Book with Online Self-Study and Online Workbook 4
ISBN 978-1-108-56029-0 Student's Book with Online Self-Study and Online Workbook 4A
ISBN 978-1-108-56032-0 Student's Book with Online Self-Study and Online Workbook 4B
ISBN 978-1-108-45942-6 Workbook 4
ISBN 978-1-108-45945-7 Workbook 4A
ISBN 978-1-108-45946-4 Workbook 4B
ISBN 978-1-108-64434-1 Teacher's Edition with Complete Assessment Program 4
ISBN 978-1-108-56022-1 Full Contact with Online Self-Study 4
ISBN 978-1-108-56023-8 Full Contact with Online Self-Study 4A
ISBN 978-1-316-56024-5 Full Contact with Online Self-Study 4B
ISBN 978-1-108-45952-5 Presentation Plus Level 4

Additional resources for this publication at www.cambridge.org/fourcorners

Authors' acknowledgments

Many people contributed to the development of *Four Corners*. The authors and publisher would like to particularly thank the following **reviewers:**

Nele Noe, **Academy for Educational Development, Qatar Independent Secondary School for Girls**, Doha, Qatar; Pablo Stucchi, **Antonio Raimondi School** and **Instituto San Ignacio de Loyola**, Lima, Peru; Nadeen Katz, **Asia University,** Tokyo, Japan; Tim Vandenhoek, **Asia University**, Tokyo, Japan; Celso Frade and Sonia Maria Baccari de Godoy, **Associação Alumni**, São Paulo, Brazil; Rosane Bandeira, **Atlanta Idiomas**, Manaus, Brazil; Cacilda Reis da Silva, **Atlanta Idiomas**, Manaus, Brazil; Gretta Sicsu, **Atlanta Idiomas**, Manaus, Brazil; Naila Maria Cañiso Ferreira, **Atlanta Idiomas**, Manaus, Brazil; Hothnã Moraes de Souza Neto, **Atlanta Idiomas**, Manaus, Brazil; Jacqueline Kurtzious, **Atlanta Idiomas**, Manaus, Brazil; José Menezes Ribeiro Neto, **Atlanta Idiomas**, Manaus, Brazil; Sheila Ribeiro Cordeiro, **Atlanta Idiomas**, Manaus, Brazil; Juliana Fernandes, **Atlanta Idiomas**, Manaus, Brazil; Aline Alexandrina da Silva, **Atlanta Idiomas**, Manaus, Brazil; Kari Miller, **Binational Center**, Quito, Ecuador; Alex K. Oliveira, **Boston University**, Boston, MA, USA; Noriko Furuya, **Bunka Gakuen University**, Tokyo, Japan; Robert Hickling, **Bunka Gakuen University**, Tokyo, Japan; John D. Owen, **Bunka Gakuen University**, Tokyo, Japan; Elisabeth Blom, **Casa Thomas Jefferson**, Brasília, Brazil; Lucilena Oliveira Andrade, **Centro Cultural Brasil Estados Unidos (CCBEU Belém)**, Belém, Brazil; Marcelo Franco Borges, **Centro Cultural Brasil Estados Unidos (CCBEU Belém)**, Belém, Brazil; Geysa de Azevedo Moreira, **Centro Cultural Brasil Estados Unidos (CCBEU Belém)**, Belém, Brazil; Anderson Felipe Barbosa Negrão, **Centro Cultural Brasil Estados Unidos (CCBEU Belém)**, Belém, Brazil; Henry Grant, **CCBEU – Campinas**, Campinas, Brazil; Maria do Rosário, **CCBEU – Franca**, Franca, Brazil; Ane Cibele Palma, **CCBEU Inter Americano**, Curitiba, Brazil; Elen Flavia Penques da Costa, **Centro de Cultura Idiomas – Taubaté**, Taubaté, Brazil; Inara Lúcia Castillo Couto, **CEL LEP – São Paulo**, São Paulo, Brazil; Sonia Patricia Cardoso, **Centro de Idiomas Universidad Manuela Beltrán**, Barrio Cedritos, Colombia; Geraldine Itiago Losada, **Centro Universitario Grupo Sol (Musali)**, Mexico City, Mexico; Nick Hilmers, **DePaul University**, Chicago, IL, USA; Monica L. Montemayor Menchaca, **EDIMSA**, Metepec, Mexico; Angela Whitby, **Edu-Idiomas Language School**, Cholula, Puebla, Mexico; Mary Segovia, **El Monte Rosemead Adult School**, Rosemead, CA, USA; Dr. Deborah Aldred, **ELS Language Centers, Middle East Region**, Abu Dhabi, United Arab Emirates; Leslie Lott, **Embassy CES**, Ft. Lauderdale, FL, USA; M. Martha Lengeling, **Escuela de Idiomas**, Guanajuato, Mexico; Pablo Frias, **Escuela de Idiomas UNAPEC**, Santo Domingo, Dominican Republic; Tracy Vanderhoek, **ESL Language Center**, Toronto, Canada; Kris Vicca and Michael McCollister, **Feng Chia University**, Taichung, Taiwan; Flávia Patricia do Nascimento Martins, **First Idiomas**, Sorocaba, Brazil; Andrea Taylor, **Florida State University in Panama**, Panamá, Panama; Carlos Lizárraga González, **Groupo Educativo Angloamericano**, Mexico City, Mexico; Bo-Kyung Lee, **Hankuk University of Foreign Studies**, Seoul, South Korea; Dr. Martin Endley, **Hanyang University**, Seoul, South Korea; Mauro Luiz Pinheiro, **IBEU Ceará**, Ceará, Brazil; Ana Lúcia da Costa Maia de Almeida, **IBEU Copacabana**, Copacabana, Brazil; Maristela Silva, **ICBEU Manaus**, Manaus, Brazil; Magaly Mendes Lemos, **ICBEU São José dos Campos**, São José dos Campos, Brazil; Augusto Pelligrini Filho, **ICBEU São Luis**, São Luis, Brazil; Leonardo Mercado, **ICPNA**, Lima, Peru; Lucia Rangel Lugo, **Instituto Tecnológico de San Luis Potosí**, San Luis Potosí, Mexico; Maria Guadalupe Hernández Lozada, **Instituto Tecnológico de Tlalnepantla**, Tlalnepantla de Baz, Mexico; Karen Stewart, **International House Veracruz**, Veracruz, Mexico; Tom David, **Japan College of Foreign Languages**, Tokyo, Japan; Andy Burki, **Korea University, International Foreign Language School**, Seoul, South Korea; Jinseo Noh, **Kwangwoon University**, Seoul, South Korea; Neil Donachey, **La Salle Junior and Senior High School**, Kagoshima, Japan; Rich Hollingworth, **La Salle Junior and Senior High School**, Kagoshima, Japan; Quentin Kum, **La Salle Junior and Senior High School**, Kagoshima, Japan; Geoff Oliver, **La Salle Junior and Senior High School**, Kagoshima, Japan; Martin Williams, **La Salle Junior and Senior High School**, Kagoshima, Japan; Nadezhda Nazarenko, **Lone Star College**, Houston, TX, USA; Carolyn Ho, **Lone Star College-Cy-Fair**, Cypress, TX, USA; Kaoru Kuwajima, **Meijo University**, Nogoya, Japan; Alice Ya-fen Chou, **National Taiwan University of Science and Technology**, Taipei, Taiwan; Raymond Dreyer, **Northern Essex Community College**, Lawrence, MA, USA; Mary Keter Terzian Megale, **One Way Línguas-Suzano**, São Paulo, Brazil; B. Greg Dunne, **Osaka Shoin Women's University**, Higashi-Osaka, Japan; Robert Maran, **Osaka Shoin Women's University**, Higashi-Osaka, Japan; Bonnie Cheeseman, **Pasadena Community College** and **UCLA American Language Center**, Los Angeles, CA, USA; Simon Banha, **Phil Young's English School**, Curitiba, Brazil; Oh Jun Il, **Pukyong National University**, Busan, South Korea; Carmen Gehrke, **Quatrum English Schools**, Porto Alegre, Brazil; John Duplice, **Rikkyo University**, Tokyo, Japan; Wilzania da Silva Nascimento, **Senac**, Manaus, Brazil; Miva Silva Kingston, **Senac**, Manaus, Brazil; Lais Lima, **Senac**, Manaus, Brazil; Yuan-hsun Chuang, **Soo Chow University**, Taipei, Taiwan; Mengjiao Wu, **Shanghai Maritime University,** Shanghai, China; Wen hsiang Su, **Shih Chien University Kaohsiung Campus**, Kaohsiung, Taiwan; Lynne Kim, **Sun Moon University (Institute for Language Education)**, Cheon An City, Chung Nam, South Korea; Regina Ramalho, **Talken English School**, Curitiba, Brazil; Tatiana Mendonça, **Talken English School**, Curitiba, Brazil; Ricardo Todeschini, **Talken English School**, Curitiba, Brazil; Monica Carvalho da Rocha, **Talken English School**, Joinville, Brazil; Karina Schoene, **Talken English School**, Joinville, Brazil; Diaña Peña Munoz and Zira Kuri, **The Anglo**, Mexico City, Mexico; Christopher Modell, **Tokai University**, Tokyo, Japan; Song-won Kim, **TTI (Teacher's Training Institute)**, Seoul, South Korea; Nancy Alarcón, **UNAM FES Zaragoza Language Center**, Mexico City, Mexico; Laura Emilia Fierro López, **Universidad Autónoma de Baja California**, Mexicali, Mexico; María del Rocío Domínguez Gaona, **Universidad Autónoma de Baja California**, Tijuana, Mexico; Saul Santos Garcia, **Universidad Autónoma de Nayarit**, Nayarit, Mexico;Christian Meléndez, **Universidad Católica de El Salvador**, San Salvador, El Salvador; Irasema Mora Pablo, **Universidad de Guanajuato**, Guanajuato, Mexico; Alberto Peto, **Universidad de Oaxaca**, Tehuantepec, Mexico; Carolina Rodriguez Beltan, **Universidad Manuela Beltrán, Centro Colombo Americano**, and **Universidad Jorge Tadeo Lozano**, Bogotá, Colombia; Nidia Milena Molina Rodriguez, **Universidad Manuela Beltrán** and **Universidad Militar Nueva Granada**, Bogotá, Colombia; Yolima Perez Arias, **Universidad Nacional de Colombia**, Bogotá, Colombia; Héctor Vázquez García, **Universidad Nacional Autónoma de Mexico**, Mexico City, Mexico; Pilar Barrera, **Universidad Técnica de Ambato**, Ambato, Ecuador; Doborah Hulston, **University of Regina**, Regina, Canada; Rebecca J. Shelton, **Valparaiso University, Interlink Language Center**, Valparaiso, IN, USA; Tae Lee, **Yonsei University**, Seodaemun-gu, Seoul, South Korea; Claudia Thereza Nascimento Mendes, **York Language Institute**, Rio de Janeiro, Brazil; Jamila Jenny Hakam, **ELT Consultant**, Muscat, Oman; Stephanie Smith, **ELT Consultant**, Austin, TX, USA.

Scope and sequence

LEVEL 4	Learning outcomes	Grammar	Vocabulary
Classroom language Page 2			
Unit 1 Pages 3–12			
The news A *Stories in the news* B *I totally agree.* C *Survival stories* D *Creating news*	**Students can...** ☑ tell news stories ☑ agree and disagree with opinions ☑ ask questions and talk about a news story ☑ discuss a news story	Verb tenses – statements Verb tenses – questions	News sections Actions in the news
Unit 2 Pages 13–22			
Communicating A *Language learning* B *One possibility is . . .* C *Have her message me.* D *Modern Communication*	**Students can . . .** ☑ give and discuss language-learning tips ☑ express interests ☑ offer options ☑ talk about ways of communicating ☑ discuss their communication preferences	Preset perfect continuous Verb + object + verb	Language-learning tips Communicate . . . or not?
Unit 3 Pages 23–32			
Food A *Street food* B *Sounds good to me.* C *Mix and bake* D *Future food*	**Students can . . .** ☑ describe ways food is prepared ☑ give and accept recommendations ☑ describe steps in a recipe ☑ discuss what people may eat in the future	Present passive Time clauses	Food preparation Tastes and textures
Unit 4 Pages 33–42			
Behavior A *The right thing to do* B *I didn't realize that.* C *Doing things differently* D *Acts of kindness*	**Students can . . .** ☑ discuss how they would react to situations ☑ express and acknowledge expectations ☑ talk about past hypothetical situations ☑ discuss ways to be kind	Second conditional Past modals for hypothetical situations	Polite and impolite behavior Word partners
Unit 5 Pages 43–52			
Travel and tourism A *Cities* B *I'll let someone know.* C *Travel experiences* D *My town, the best town*	**Students can . . .** ☑ make comparisons about cities ☑ report and respond to a problem ☑ report commands and advice ☑ discuss ideas for a festival in their town	Comparatives and superlatives Reporting commands and advice	Compound adjectives Travel talk
Unit 6 Pages 53–62			
The way we are A *Who I am* B *Sorry, but can I ask something?* C *Wishing for change* D *Alternative therapies*	**Students can . . .** ☑ talk about character traits ☑ interrupt politely ☑ agree to an interruption ☑ talk about present wishes ☑ discuss ways to relax	Defining relative clauses *Wish*	Character traits Tips to manage stress

Functional language	Listening and Pronunciation	Reading and Writing	Speaking
Interactions: Agreeing with an opinion Disagreeing politely	**Listening:** Today's news News reports based on viewer-submitted photos **Pronunciation:** Reduced vowel sounds	**Reading:** "Citizen Journalism" A magazine article **Writing:** Become a citizen journalist	• Information exchange about news stories • *Keep talking:* Interview about news-reading habits • Opinions on reading the news • Information exchange about headline news • *Keep talking:* Board game to practice questions • A news blog
Interactions: Expressing interest Offering opinions	**Listening:** Options for English classes Favorite methods of communication **Pronunciation:** Unreleased final consonant sounds	**Reading:** "Too Much Information" A magazine article **Writing:** A conversation in writing	• Discussion of improving English to communicate successfully • *Keep talking:* "Find someone who" activity about recent experiences • Role play about language class options • Personal anecdotes about communicating • *Keep talking:* Role play of body language • Class survey about most popular ways of communicating
Interactions: Giving a recommendation Accepting a recommendation	**Listening:** Healthy eating habits The San Francisco Gourmet Chocolate Tour **Pronunciation:** Linked consonant and vowel sounds	**Reading:** "What Will You Be Eating 25 Years from Today?" A magazine article **Writing:** A recipe	• List of popular street foods • *Keep talking:* Description of festival foods • Role play about finding time to cook • Description of an original snack • *Keep talking:* Interview about fun food facts • A plan for a food tour
Interactions: Expressing an expectation Acknowledging an expectation	**Listening:** Cross-cultural differences Radio talk show about acts of kindness **Pronunciation:** Reduction of *have*	**Reading:** "Make Someone Happy" A magazine article **Writing:** An act of kindness	• Interviews about reactions to different situations • *Keep talking:* Information exchange about reaction to dilemmas • Information exchange about customs in different countries • Information exchange about past hypothetical situations • *Keep talking:* Discussion of right and wrong decisions • Discussion about kind acts
Interactions: Reporting a problem Responding to a problem	**Listening:** Hotel problems City festivals **Pronunciation:** Linking of same consonant sounds	**Reading:** "Welcome to Medellin, Columbia – The City of Everlasting Spring" A website **Writing:** Creating a home page	• Comparison of different cities • *Keep talking:* Travel adventure game • Role play about a hotel situation • Advice for foreign visitors • *Keep talking:* Interview about solutions to travel problems • A plan for a town festival
Interactions: Interrupting politely Agreeing to an interruption	**Listening:** Type A and Type B personalities Guided imagery **Pronunciation:** Stress in thought groups	**Reading:** "Therapies That Work!" An article **Writing:** About relaxation	• Discussion about job and personality matches • *Keep talking:* Discussion of birth order and personality • Discussion about personality • Information exchange about making wishes • *Keep talking:* Board game about wishes • Brainstorm creative ways to relax

LEVEL 4	Learning outcomes	Grammar	Vocabulary
Unit 7 Pages 63–72			
New ways of thinking A *Inventions* B *Got any suggestions?* C *Accidental inventions* D *Making life easier*	**Students can . . .** ☑ describe important inventions ☑ elicit ideas ☑ suggesting solutions ☑ discuss how things have been improved ☑ describe something they invented	*So* and *such* The passive	Positive and negative descriptions Verb and noun formation
Unit 8 Pages 73–82			
Lessons in life A *Why did I do that?* B *I'm sure you'll do fine.* C *What if . . . ?* D *A day to remember*	**Students can . . .** ☑ describe events in the past ☑ express worry ☑ reassure someone ☑ talk about how things might have been ☑ describe a memorable day	Past perfect Third conditional	Prefixes: *mis-*, *dis-*, and *re-* Expression with *make* and *get*
Unit 9 Pages 83–92			
Can you believe it? A *Everyday explanations* B *I'm pretty sure that . . .* C *History's mysteries* D *Unexplained abilities*	**Students can . . .** ☑ speculate about everyday situations ☑ express probability and improbability ☑ ask and speculate about historical events ☑ discuss the power of memory	Past modals for speculating Embedded questions	Suffixes *-ful* and *-less* Mysterious events
Unit 10 Pages 93–102			
Perspectives A *A traffic accident* B *As I was saying . . .* C *There's always an explanation* D *Seeing things differently*	**Students can . . .** ☑ report what people say ☑ change and return to the topic ☑ report what people ask ☑ discuss different perspectives	Reported statements Reported *yes / no* questions	Three-word phrasal verbs Verbs + prepositions
Unit 11 Pages 103–112			
The real world A *Getting it done* B *Let me see . . .* C *Future goals* D *My career*	**Students can . . .** ☑ talk about getting things done ☑ take time to think in an interview ☑ close an interview ☑ ask and talk about future goals ☑ discuss future careers	Causative *get* and *have* Future continuous vs. future with *will*	Word partners Setting goals
Unit 12 Pages 113–122			
Finding solutions A *Environmental concerns* B *That's a good point.* C *My community* D *Getting involved*	**Students can . . .** ☑ discuss environmental trends ☑ support and not support an opinion ☑ discuss ways to improve their community ☑ discuss ways to raise awareness	Present continuous passive Infinitive passive Linking words	Preventing pollution Community improvement

Functional language	Listening and Pronunciation	Reading and Writing	Speaking
Interactions: Eliciting an idea Suggesting a solution	**Listening:** Unusual solutions to unusual problems i-Cybie, a robot dog **Pronunciation:** Emphatic stress	**Reading:** "Technology Helps Japan's Elderly" An article **Writing:** An Invention	• Discussion of inventions • *Keep talking:* Promoting creative products • Vote on inventive solutions • Discussion of improvements to early innovations • *Keep talking:* Discussion of product improvements • Description of an original invention
Interactions: Expressing worry Reassuring someone	**Listening:** Worrisome situations Memorable days **Pronunciation:** Reduction of had	**Reading:** "Tuesday, January 9, 2007" A magazine article **Writing:** About a memorable day	• Information exchange about past experiences • *Keep talking:* Picture story • Role play about difficult situations • Description of personal experiences that might have been different • *Keep talking:* Discussion of possible outcomes in different situations • Description of a memorable day
Interactions: Expressing probability Expressing improbability	**Listening:** Mind-reading "The Magpies and the Bell," a South Korean folktale **Pronunciation:** Intonation in embedded questions	**Reading:** "The Woman Who Can't forget" A magazine article **Writing:** An origin myth	• Discussion of possible explanations for unusual everyday events • *Keep talking:* Speculations about pictured events • Information exchange about probability • Discussion of possible explanations for historical mysteries • *Keep talking:* Descriptions and speculations about unsolved mysteries • Story-telling from different cultures
Interactions: Changing the topic Returning to a topic	**Listening:** Three conversations about sports Interview for the Proust Questionnaire **Pronunciation:** Linked vowel sounds with / w / and / y /	**Reading:** "The Dress" A lecture **Writing:** Questionnaire results	• "Whisper the sentence" game to report what people say • *Keep talking:* "Find the differences" activity about eyewitness reports • Discussion about sports • "Find someone who" activity about famous people • *Keep talking:* Survey about general topics • Questionnaire about thoughts and values
Interactions: Taking time to think Closing an interview	**Listening:** Plans to get things done A job interview **Pronunciation:** Reduction of will	**Reading:** "Jobs of the future" An article **Writing:** A letter of interest	• Discussion about ways to prepare for an interview • *Keep talking:* Match the places and the activities • Role play about a job interview • Discussion of future goals • *Keep talking:* Survey about life in the future
Interactions: Supporting an opinion Not supporting an opinion	**Listening:** Bottled water and the environment How people help solve community issues **Pronunciation:** Rise-falling and low falling tones	**Reading:** "El Sistema: Social Change Through Music" A magazine article **Writing:** A letter to a community leader	• Discussion of environmental trends • *Keep talking:* Board game about the environment • Comparison of opinions about issues • Discussion about ways to improve the quality of life of people in the community • *Keep talking:* A plan for a community improvement project • Information exchange about raising awareness

Classroom Language

A Complete the conversations with the correct sentences. Then listen and check your answers.

Do you think this is correct?	Is it all right if I . . .
✓ Do you want to join our group?	Which number are we on?
I'm sorry for being late.	Would you mind explaining that to me?

1

A Do you want to join our group?

B That'd be great. Thanks.

2

A ______________________________

B Sure. I think I understand it.

3

A ______________________________

leave five minutes early tomorrow? I have a doctor's appointment.

B Of course.

4

A ______________________________

My last class ended late.

B That's OK. Take your seat.

5

A ______________________________

B We just finished question two, so we're on number three now.

6

A ______________________________

B I don't think so. I think you need to use the past tense here.

B PAIR WORK Practice the conversations.

1 The news

LESSON A
- News sections
- Verb tenses – statements

LESSON B
- Agreeing with an opinion
- Disagreeing politely

LESSON C
- Actions in the news
- Verb tenses – questions

LESSON D
- Reading: "Citizen Journalism"
- Writing: Become a citizen journalist

Warm Up

A Look at the pictures. How are the people getting their news?

B How do people you know get the news? How do you get the news?

A Stories in the news

1 Vocabulary News sections

A **Listen to the names of news sections. In which news sections can you find the pictures? Compare your answers with a partner.**

a	Business	c	Health	e	Local	g	Technology / Science	i	Weather
b	Entertainment	✓ d	Lifestyle	f	Sports	h	Travel	j	World

1 ☐

2 ☐

3 ☐

4 ☐

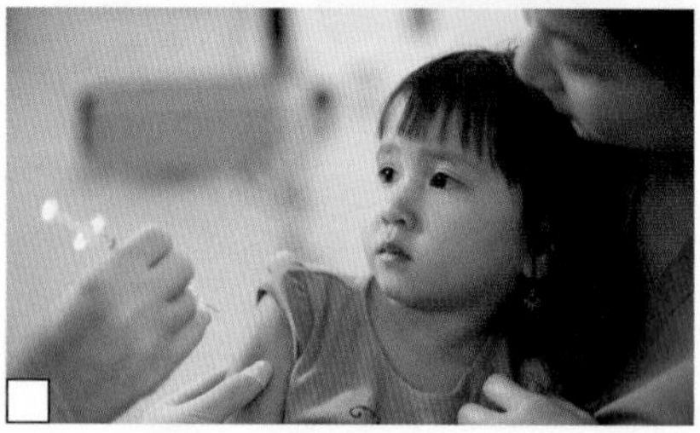
5 ☐

6 ☐

"I think you can find the first picture in the Lifestyle section."

B PAIR WORK **In which news section can you find these news stories? Discuss your ideas.**

the best new applications for phones	a meeting among world leaders
last night's soccer scores	a new coffeehouse in your town

2 Language in context In the news

A **Read the headlines and the beginning of each story. Match the headlines to the news sections in Exercise 1A where you can find these stories.**

PHOTOS SHOW ANCIENT MARTIAN LAKE _____ ☐

New photos suggest that Mars had a large lake billions of years ago.

Town Recovering from Storm _____ ☐

The town of Jasper is slowly recovering from last week's storm.

OPEN FOR BUSINESS _____ ☐

Hawaii hopes to attract more business travelers.

Jason Parker Debuts New Visual Album at Lucid's _____ ☐

Jason was playing his new songs and videos to an excited audience until 2:00 a.m.

B **What about you? Are you interested in these stories? Rank them from 1 to 4 in the order you would read them.**

3 Grammar Verb tenses – statements

Simple present:	Hawaii **hopes** to attract more business travelers.
Present continuous:	Jasper **is recovering** from last week's storm.
Simple past:	Mars **had** a large lake billions of years ago.
Past continuous:	Jason **was playing** songs all night.
Present perfect:	Café Bella **has opened** in Pelham.
Future with will:	The Winter Olympics **will begin** next Monday.

Complete the news stories with the correct forms of the verbs. Then compare with a partner.

1 The *Austin Sun Times* ___has closed___ (close) its doors – for now. The newspaper ________ (print) its last newspaper last Sunday, but it ________ (open) again next month as an Internet-only paper. Staff members ________ (learn) about digital publishing now, so they ________ (be) ready next month. Sadly, the *Austin Gazette* ________ (be) now the city's only "paper" newspaper.

2 Pink ________ (be) a playful color, and it ________ (make) people smile. But last night William Maddox ________ (not / smile) when he ________ (stop) a fight in his store. "Two people ________ (argue) for about five minutes over the last pink T-shirt in my store. I ________ (ask) them to leave and then ________ (close) the store for the day," said Maddox.

3 Fifteen-year-old Kate Moore ________ (be) the country's newest coding champion. Last Tuesday, she ________ (compete) against 20 other contestants and ________ (win) $50,000 for her fast and accurate coding. Kate ________ (get) everything right. "No one ________ (know) how to solve one of the Math problems, except me! Winning ________ (mean) a lot to me. My parents ________ (watch)."

4 Speaking News stories

A PAIR WORK **Think of a story from the news, or make one up. Complete the chart.**

What happened?	
What else was happening at the time?	
What has happened since?	
What's happening now?	

B GROUP WORK **Share your stories. What will happen in the future?**

5 Keep talking!

Go to page 123 for more practice.

I can tell news stories.

B I totally agree.

1 Interactions Agreeing and disagreeing

A **Do you agree with this statement? Why or why not?**

"The best place to get news is online."

B **Listen to the conversation. Why can't Carl check the news headlines? Then practice the conversation.**

Carl Hey, Jim. Catching up on the news?

Jim Oh, hi, Carl. Yeah, I like to know what's going on in the world.

Carl I feel exactly the same way. Do you read the paper every day?

Jim Every day. It's the best way to get the news.

Carl Really? I don't know about that. I get all my news online. I check the news several times a day, so I always know what's happening.

Jim Online news is OK, but I prefer reading an actual newspaper. So, what are the latest headlines online – right now?

Carl Let's see. . . . Oh, no! I can't get online. I guess there's no wireless signal here. Say, would you mind sharing your paper?

Jim No problem!

C **Read the expressions below. Complete each box with a similar expression from the conversation. Then listen and check your answers.**

Agreeing with an opinion	Disagreeing politely
______________________	______________________
I couldn't agree with you more.	I'm not sure about that.
I totally agree.	I'm not sure that's really true.

D **PAIR WORK** **Check (✓) the statements you agree with. Then give your opinions and agree or disagree with your partner.**

- ☐ It's important to read the news every day.
- ☐ The Internet is a better way to get news than newspapers.
- ☐ Social media is a good way to get news.
- ☐ There's not enough positive news these days.

A: *I think it's important to read the news every day.*

B: *I totally agree. It's important to know what's going on.*

2 Pronunciation Reduced vowel sounds

A **Listen and repeat. Notice the reduced vowel sound /ə/ in unstressed syllables.**

agree totally even happening

B **Listen. Underline the reduced vowel sounds. Then practice with a partner.**

signal about magazine travel section television

3 Listening Agree or disagree

A **Listen to Ted and Carrie discuss today's news. What news are they talking about? Number the pictures from 1 to 4.**

B **Listen again. Does Carrie agree or disagree with Ted? Circle the answers.**

1 agree / disagree 2 agree / disagree 3 agree / disagree 4 agree / disagree

4 Speaking What do you think?

A **Check (✓) the statements you agree with, and mark an ✗ next to the statements you disagree with. Then write a supporting sentence for your opinion.**

Statement	Supporting sentence
☐ News bloggers don't provide real news.	
☐ International news stories don't affect me.	
☐ It's important to follow local news.	
☐ Getting news 24 hours a day is helpful.	
☐ Newspapers hurt the environment.	

B CLASS ACTIVITY **Walk around the class. Share your opinions with your classmates. Agree or disagree politely.**

A: In my opinion, news bloggers don't provide real news. They write opinions, not facts.

B: I'm not sure that's true. A lot of bloggers are really newspaper writers.

I can agree and disagree with opinions.

C Survival stories

1 Vocabulary Actions in the news

A 🎧 **Match the news headlines and the pictures. Then listen and check your answers.**

a	Shark **Attacks** Local Surfer	e	Boat **Overturns** – All Swim to Safety
b	Bear **Chases** Hiker Up Tree	f	Firefighter **Rescues** Family Cat
c	Pilot **Crashes** Plane – No One Hurt	g	Hiker **Survives** Week in the Mountains
d	Lightning **Misses** Golfer by One Foot	h	Fire **Threatens** Historic Town

1 

2 

3 

4 

5 

6 

7 

8 

B PAIR WORK **Use each verb in Part A in a new headline.**

"Swimmer Survives Three Days in Ocean"

2 Conversation Shark attack!

A 🎧 **Listen to the conversation. How did Wade stop the shark?**

Reporter: Wade, what happened?

Wade: A shark attacked me! Can you believe it?

Reporter: How are you feeling? Are you OK?

Wade: Oh, I feel great! I survived a shark attack. That's pretty cool.

Reporter: What were you doing when it happened?

Wade: I was riding a killer wave.

Reporter: Did you actually see the shark?

Wade: Not at first. But then I fell off my board. The shark tried to bite me, so I hit it with my surfboard.

Reporter: Have you seen your surfboard?

Wade: Yeah. It has a big shark bite in it.

Reporter: Amazing! So, what will you do next?

B 🎧 **Listen to the rest of the interview. What will Wade do next? When?**

3 Grammar Verb tenses – questions

	Wh- questions	*Yes / no* questions
Simple present:	When **do** you **plan** on surf ing?	**Do** you **plan** on surfing today?
Present continuous:	How **are** you **feeling**?	**Are** you **feeling** OK?
Simple past:	What **did** you **see**?	**Did** you **see** the shark?
Past continuous:	What **were** you **doing**?	**Were** you **surfing**?
Present perfect:	How long **have** you **surfed**?	**Have** you **surfed** for a long time?
Future with will:	What **will** you **do** next?	**Will** you **go** back in the water soon?

A Look at the *yes / no* questions the reporter asked Wade. Complete the questions with the correct forms of the verbs. Then compare with a partner.

1 ______ you ______ (go) surfing every day?
2 ______ anyone ______ (see) the shark before it attacked you?
3 ______ other people ______ (surf) around you?
4 ______ you ______ (buy) a new surfboard soon?
5 ______ you ______ (speak) with your family yet?
6 ______ you ______ (have) any advice for other surfers?

B Read the answers. Write *Wh-* questions about the underlined words. Then practice with a partner.

1 *Where did she crash the plane?* She crashed the plane in a forest.
2 ______ He's been in the desert for a week.
3 ______ The firefighter felt very proud.
4 ______ The fire will threaten the town center tonight.
5 ______ They were fishing when the boat overturned.
6 ______ He's thinking about writing a survival book.

4 Speaking Tell me about it.

PAIR WORK **Role-play a reporter and a survivor of one of the news stories in Exercise 1. Then change roles.**

Student A: Choose a headline from Exercise 1, and read it to your partner. Answer your partner's questions.

Student B: Ask your partner five questions about what happened.

A: Who were you sailing with?

B: I was sailing with some friends.

Questions
1. Who were you sailing with?
2. How exactly did the boat overturn?
3. How often do you go sailing?
4. Have you ever . . . ?
5.

5 Keep talking!

Go to page 124 for more practice.

I can ask questions and talk about a news story.

D Creating news

1 Reading

A **Look at the logos of the news websites in the article. Which websites have you looked at? What other news websites do you know?**

B **Read the article. Check (✓) the main idea of the article.**

- ☐ Traditional news organizations are upset with citizen journalists.
- ☐ Technology allows anyone to be a reporter, anytime and anywhere.

Citizen Journalism

Arpita has just updated her news blog.

The winners of a local election in Mumbai have just been announced, and she has listed their names on her blog. On the website of a local newspaper, Liat has recently posted a "digital story," a series of photos a descriptions of a whale rescue. And hundreds of people in the Dominican Republic are tweeting on their ce phones to describe a hurricane that is threatening the country.

What do these stories have in common? Technology is giving people the chance to be news reporters. More than ever before, technology is allowing everyone to share opinions, ideas, stories, photos, and videos from anywhere in the world. If there is **breaking news**, you can be sure that someone is reporting

GroundReport, CNN's iReport, and Blufftontoday.com are just a few of the websites where "citizen journalists" can post their articles, photos, or videos. More and more people are making Youtube chann Instagram, or Snapchat profiles that get more than one million views!

They're sharing their personal thoughts and news reports with the world on these websites. And the increased **prevalence** of cell phones and cameras has made it even easier for people to share content.

Many media organizations such as CNN now have entire sections of these news stories on their websi News editors used to decide what was news. Now *you* decide.

There has been some **criticism** of citizen journalism, however. For example, there are often mistakes in these stories, including incorrect facts, spelling, grammar, or even news that is fake! These stories may no be as **reliable** as regular news organizations' stories usually are. Moreover, when people **instantly** upload stories and images, they cannot know how other people will use them later. But it seems that news by the people and for the people is here to stay.

C **Find the words in bold in the article. Circle the correct meaning.**

1	**breaking news**	a. news happening now	b. news about problems
2	**prevalence**	a. lower cost of	b. frequent use
3	**criticism**	a. high costs	b. opinions on what's wrong
4	**reliable**	a. written well	b. trustworthy
5	**instantly**	a. immediately	b. done without thinking

D **What's your opinion about citizen journalism? Do you think it's a good thing? Do you agree with the criticisms in the article? Do you have other ideas?**

2 Listening Photos of the day

A 🎧 **Listen to a TV newscaster discuss photos that four viewers have sent in. Number the photos from 1 to 4.**

B 🎧 **Listen again. Answer the questions.**

1 When did Rafael take the photograph?

2 How much of a discount was the store offering?

3 How long does it usually take Yumiko to get home?

4 What did Arlo do when he saw the animal?

C **Which news stories in Part A interest you? Why? Where can you find out more about them?**

3 Writing and speaking Become a citizen journalist

A **Complete one of these headlines.**

HUGE STORM TO ARRIVE ______

______ Threatens High School

LOCAL TEEN RESCUES ______ IN FOREST

Lightning Misses ______

Technology Changes ______

Students Ask ______ for ______

B **Write a short news blog. Use your headline from Part A and the model to help you.**

Huge Storm to Arrive Friday

A huge storm is coming on Friday. Everyone is preparing for it. Most people have already bought food and water. . .

C GROUP WORK **Share your news blogs. Ask questions to find out more information about each story.**

I can discuss a news story. ✓

Wrap-up

1 Quick pair review

Lesson A Find out!

What are two sections of the news both you and your partner like to read? You and your partner have one minute.

A: I read the World section of the newspaper. Do you?

B: No, I don't. I read the Travel section. Do you?

A: Yes, I do.

Lesson B Do you remember?

Write A for expressions that show agreeing with an opinion and D for expressions that show disagreeing with an opinion. You have one minute.

A 1 I feel exactly the same way.

___ 2 I couldn't agree with you more.

___ 3 I'm not sure about that.

___ 4 I don't know about that.

___ 5 I totally agree.

___ 6 I'm not sure that's really true.

Lesson C Brainstorm!

Write the question "Where do you shop?" in as many different tenses as you can. You have two minutes.

Lesson D Guess!

Describe something newsworthy for each item, but don't say where it happened. Can your partner guess the place? Take turns. You and your partner have three minutes.

something you did yesterday
something you do every day
something you will do tomorrow

A: Yesterday I ate at a great café. I had tacos and rice and beans.

B: Were you at Café Mexicana?

A: Yes, I was.

2 In the real world

What is a breaking news story in your area? Go online or read a newspaper, and find an article in English about it. Then write about it.

- What section did you find the article in?
- What happened?

Oil Spill Threatens Animals

The national news reported an oil spill in the Gulf of Mexico. The oil will harm fish and birds.

2 Communicating

LESSON A

- Language-learning tips
- Present perfect continuous

LESSON B

- Expressing interest
- Offering options

LESSON C

- Communicate . . . or not?
- Verb + object + verb

LESSON D

- Reading: "Too Much Information"
- Writing: A conversation in writing

Warm Up

A Look at the pictures. What do you think the people are saying?

B Imagine you are going to travel to an English-speaking country. What do you think are the most useful English phrases or questions to know? Why?

A Language learning

1 Vocabulary Language-learning tips

A Complete the chart with the correct tips. Then listen and check your answers.

Tips for Successful Language Learning

- Watch online video clips.
- Keep a vocabulary notebook.
- ✓ Make flash cards.
- Talk with native speakers.
- Watch movies with subtitles.
- Talk to yourself out loud.

To remember vocabulary
Make flash cards.
To increase speaking fluency
To improve listening comprehension

B PAIR WORK What's your number one language-learning goal? Which tips in Part A do you use to reach your goal? Tell your partner.

"My number one goal is to improve my listening comprehension. I often watch online video clips in English."

2 Language in context Improving communication skills

A Read this online chat between a teacher and some of his students. What are they discussing?

Group Chat

Mr. Phillips, Luisa, Jin, Marcus, Pe...

Mr. Phillips I hope you've been enjoying your vacation. And I hope you haven't forgotten your English! So, what have you been doing recently to improve your English?

Luisa Hello, Mr. Phillips. Hi, everybody! I've been reading magazines and comic books in English.

Mr. Phillips Excellent!

Jin I've been making vocabulary flash cards. They really work! And I've been keeping a vocabulary notebook.

Marcus I've been chatting online in English.

Mr. Phillips Fantastic! Have you been doing anything to improve your speaking?

Pedro I have. Omar and I have been starting conversations with native speakers. We were nervous about it at first, but we've been making new friends that way.

Luisa I've been having the best conversations of all. I've been talking to myself out loud in front of a mirror.

Marcus Very funny!

Mr. Phillips But very helpful, too. Good job, everyone! I'll see you in class on Monday.

B What about you? Which tips would you like to try? Which would you probably not want to try? Why?

3 Grammar Present perfect continuous

Use the present perfect continuous to emphasize the duration of an action that is in progress. How long, recently, *and* lately *are often used with the present perfect continuous.*

What **have** you **been doing** recently?
I**'ve been reading** magazines.

How long **has** he **been writing** in his notebook?
He**'s been writing** in it for about a month.

Have they **been talking** to native speakers lately?
Yes, they **have**. No, they **haven't**.

Remember: some verbs are not usually used in the continuous form.

believe	like
belong	love
forget	need
hate	own
hope	remember
know	want

A Complete the conversations with the present perfect continuous forms of the verbs. Then practice with a partner.

1 A ________ you ________ (do) anything recently to improve your vocabulary?
B Yes, I ________. I ________ (keep) a vocabulary notebook.

2 A How long ________ you ________ (study) English?
B I ________ (study) English since last year.

3 A What ________ you ________ (do) in class lately?
B We ________ (make) vocabulary flash cards.

B PAIR WORK Ask the questions in Part A. Answer with your own information.

4 Speaking Communicating successfully

A GROUP WORK What have these people been doing lately to improve their English? What language goals do you think they have been trying to reach?

B CLASS ACTIVITY What else can you do to improve your speaking? Learn more vocabulary? Improve listening comprehension? Discuss your ideas and make a class list of tips.

5 Keep talking!

Go to page 125 for more practice.

I can give and discuss language-learning tips.

B One possibility is . . .

1 Interactions Interests and options

A **How good is your English? Rate these areas 1 (good), 2 (fair), or 3 (not very good).**

- ☐ reading ☐ writing ☐ speaking ☐ listening
- ☐ vocabulary ☐ grammar ☐ pronunciation ☐ idioms

B **Listen to the conversation. What idiom did Ralph learn? Then practice the conversation.**

Ralph Excuse me. Do you have a minute?

Mr. Hill Of course, Ralph. What's up?

Ralph Well, I'm trying to find a way to learn English idioms. Can you help me?

Mr. Hill Well, how about taking one of our conversation courses? I know Ms. Davis teaches a lot of idioms.

Ralph OK.

Mr. Hill But why are you so interested in idioms?

Ralph Oh, a friend and I were making plans, and he said, "Let's play it by ear." I asked him to repeat it, but I still didn't understand.

Mr. Hill I see. Well, "play it by ear" means you don't make plans ahead of time. You decide what seems best at the time.

Ralph Oh, I know that now. I looked it up online. But that's why I need to learn idioms.

C **Read the expressions below. Complete each box with a similar expression from the conversation. Then listen and check your answers.**

Expressing interest	Offering options
________________	________________
I'm interested in . . .	One possibility is . . .
I'm looking for . . .	You might want to consider . . .

D **PAIR WORK** **Express interest in improving your skills in one of the areas in Part A. Your partner offers course options. Take turns.**

Podcasting in English	Advanced Grammar	Academic Test Prep
Vocabulary for Science	Intermediate Listening	Pronunciation Workshop

2 Pronunciation Unreleased final consonant sounds

A 🎧 **Listen and repeat. Notice how the final sounds /b/, /g/, /d/, /p/,/k/, and /t/ are not fully pronounced before other consonant sounds.**

Film Club Group Discussions	Advanced Grammar	Travel Blog Writing
Intermediate Conversation	Academic Listening	Test Prep Course

B 🎧 **Listen. Cross out the final sounds that are not fully pronounced. Then practice with a partner.**

Create flash cards.	Set realistic goals.	Join group discussions.
Read books in English.	Memorize verb tenses.	Write a blog for practice.

3 Listening Fun classes

A 🎧 **Listen to a man ask about options for English classes. Write the class names.**

	Class name	One interesting thing
1		
2		
3		
4		

B 🎧 **Listen again. Write one interesting thing about each class. Then circle the class the man chooses.**

4 Speaking Consider all the options!

PAIR WORK **Role-play the situation. Then change roles.**

Student A: You are a new student at a language school. Student B has been taking classes at the school for a year. Ask about class options and choose one.

Student B: You have been taking classes at your language school for a year. Student A is a new student. Help Student A find the right class from the classes below.

Academic Listening	Vocabulary for Science	Reading for Business	Advanced Speaking
Tue. & Thur., 4:00–6:00 p.m.	Mon. & Fri., 7:00–8:30 a.m.	Wed., 2:00–5:00 p.m.	Tue. & Thur., 6:00–8:00 p.m.
Practice note-taking and intensive listening.	Learn science vocabulary and academic skills.	Practice reading notes, memos, and reports.	Improve your speaking skills.

A: *I'm interested in a way to improve my reading.*

B: *One class possibility is Reading for Business. They practice reading memos.*

A: *Really? I don't know about that. . . .*

I can express interests. ✓

I can offer options. ✓

C Have her message me.

1 Vocabulary Communicate . . . or not?

A 🎧 **Label the phrases C (ways to communicate) or A (ways to avoid communicating). Then listen and check your answers.**

1 answer the phone _C_
2 call (someone) back ______
3 don't check voice mail ______
4 ignore a text ______
5 leave (someone) a voice message ______
6 let the call go to voice mail ______
7 respond to an email ______
8 screen your calls ______
9 turn off the phone ______
10 update your status online ______

B PAIR WORK **How do you usually communicate? What things do you sometimes do to avoid communicating?**

"I update my status online every day. That way my friends know what I'm doing."

2 Conversation Where's Beth?

A 🎧 **Listen to the conversation. How has Pete been trying to contact Beth?**

Akemi Hello?
Pete Hi, Akemi. It's Pete.
Akemi Oh, hi, Pete. How are things?
Pete Good, thanks. Listen, have you seen Beth? I've left her a lot of voice messages, but she hasn't returned my calls.
Akemi That's strange. Maybe she's busy and just isn't checking her voice mail.
Pete She's probably screening her calls. It's too bad, because I really need to ask her to help me with something.
Akemi Have you tried emailing her?
Pete Several times, but so far she's ignored my emails – and my texts.
Akemi That's not like her. You know, I usually see her at the gym on Sundays.
Pete Oh, really? Could you ask her to call me back or to message me?
Akemi Sure, I can do that.

B 🎧 **Listen to a conversation between Pete and Beth. Why hasn't Beth been answering her phone? What's Pete planning?**

3 Grammar Verb + object + verb

Some verbs are commonly followed by an object and the base form of another verb.	*Some verbs are commonly followed by an object and an infinitive (to + verb).*
Would you **let** me **help**?	I **invited** you **to come**.
Please **make** them **be** quiet.	I'll **ask** her **to help** me.
Could you **have** her **message** me?	Would you **tell** her **to call** me?
Please **help** me **call** people.	Could you **remind** them **to come** early?

A Circle the correct forms of the verbs. Then compare with a partner.

1 You're talking to a friend on the phone and you get another call. What do you do?
  a. I tell the caller **call** / **to call** me back later.
  b. I have my friend **call** / **to call** me back.

2 Your grandmother can't input numbers into her cell phone. What do you do?
  a. I have someone **input** / **to input** the numbers for her.
  b. I say, "Let me **help** / **to help** you."

3 Your phone rings in the middle of the night. What do you do?
  a. I let the call **go** / **to go** to voice mail.
  b. I answer but ask the person **call** / **to call** back in the morning.

4 An uninvited stranger shows up at your party. What do you do?
  a. I invite the person **come** / **to come** in.
  b. I make the person **leave** / **to leave**.

5 A friend is always phoning you in class. What do you do?
  a. I remind my friend **call** / **to call** later.
  b. I ask my friend **stop** / **to stop** calling.

6 Your sister has been secretly using your phone to send texts. What do you do?
  a. I make her **pay** / **to pay** for using my phone.
  b. I let her **continue** / **to continue** to use my phone.

B PAIR WORK **Ask and answer the questions in Part A. Make the answers true for you.**

4 Speaking Chat about it.

GROUP WORK **Answer the questions. Give more information.**

1 Do you ever get texts, emails, or calls from companies trying to sell things? What do you do to make them stop calling?
2 Has your computer or phone ever stopped working? Did you have someone fix it for you? Who?
3 Would you let a stranger borrow your phone? Do you ever ask to borrow someone's phone? When?
4 Have you ever sent an email to the wrong person? Who did you send it to? Did this person respond to your email? What did he or she say?

"I sometimes get calls from companies. I ask them to stop calling."

5 Keep talking!

Go to pages 126–127 for more practice.

I can talk about ways of communicating.

D Modern communication

1 Reading

A **Read the first paragraph of the article. What is "communication overload"?**

TOO MUCH INFORMATION

Computers and cell phones let people communicate with each other by voice or text anytime, anywhere. The result: too much information! So let me offer these tips. They could help you manage communication overload.

TIP 1 – *Stick to a schedule.* Do you have a calendar? Use it to schedule study times, meetings, and appointments. But also, use it to schedule times to respond to email, read status updates, and check your messages. How about also using it to schedule quiet time? That is, **set aside** time for no email, no texts, no phone calls, nothing! Then **stick to it**!

TIP 2 – *Text or phone call?* Texts are great for short messages, but not for long messages with emotional **content**. Phone calls are fine when you want a more personal touch, but not when you need to save information about a conversation. In those cases, an email or a letter may be better.

TIP 3 – *Let it ring.* You don't have to answer every phone call. If you don't want to talk, screen your calls and let the caller leave a message. Or turn off your phone. The same is true for text messages. It's usually OK to make people wait for your answer.

TIP 4 – *Keep your in-box empty.* After you've answered an email, delete it or file it. If you need to save an email, create folders – for school, for work, for friends. Find a way to organize your messages that works for you, and follow it.

TIP 5 – *Pick one primary network.* Many people have a **profile** on a social network site, like Facebook. Some people have profiles on many different sites. Choose one site as your **primary** place to communicate with people. Keep your profiles on the other sites, but check those sites less frequently.

TIP 6 – *Choose your friends carefully.* If you belong to a social network site, are all your "friends" on the site real friends and family, or are some just **casual acquaintances** or even strangers? Limit the number of "friends" you welcome into your social network, and you will limit communication overload from people you don't care about.

B **Read the article. Find the words in bold. What do they mean? Write the words next to the correct definition.**

1 main primary
2 continue to do it ______
3 people you don't know well ______
4 save for later ______
5 information about yourself ______
6 subject matter ______

C **Check (✓) the statements the author would probably agree with.**

- ☐ It's always better to call.
- ☐ It's OK to be on more than one social network site.
- ☐ Create several email folders.
- ☐ You should always communicate with people.

D **Do you think you suffer from communication overload? Why or why not?**

2 Listening Communication preferences

A Listen to four friends describe their favorite method of communicating. Write the method each person prefers.

	Method	Why he or she prefers it
Lynn		☐ It's fast, cheap, and easy. ☐ She dislikes checking her voice mail.
Alex		☐ He forgets to answer texts. ☐ He can talk to the person right away.
Anita		☐ She can communicate with a lot of people at the same time. ☐ She can see what her friends are doing.
Dean		☐ It's more personal. ☐ He can respond to email by phone.

B Listen again. Check (✓) why they prefer their method of communication.

3 Writing A conversation in writing

A Write an answer to the question "What's the best way to communicate with people?" Use the model to help you.

B GROUP WORK Pass your answer to the classmate on your right. Read and respond to your classmate's answer. Continue to pass, read, and respond to all of the answers in your group.

C Read the answers and responses. Which way to communicate is the best?

Ming: The best way to communicate with people is to talk in person.
Ella: I don't think so. Sometimes people are too far away.
Justine: Then one possibility is calling the person to talk.
Eduardo: I'm not sure about that. . . .

4 Speaking How I communicate

A GROUP WORK Answer the questions. Give more information.

- What is your primary way of communicating?
- Who do you use it to communicate with?
- What do you like about it? Is there anything you dislike about it?
- Has your way of communicating with people changed in the past year? How?
- Do you think you'll still use this method in one year? Five years? Why or why not?

"I usually use my phone. I talk to everyone this way. . . ."

B CLASS ACTIVITY Take a class survey. What's the most popular way of communicating among your classmates?

I can discuss my communication preferences. ✓

Wrap-up

1 Quick pair review

Lesson A Test your partner!

Say three sentences in the present continuous. Can your partner say them correctly in the present perfect continuous? Take turns. You and your partner have two minutes.

A: *I'm reading a good book.*

B: *I've been reading a good book lately.*

Lesson B Do you remember?

Complete the sentences with the correct phrases to express interest and offer options. Write the letter of the correct phrase. You have two minutes.

1 A I'm interested ______
B You might want to consider ______
2 A I'm looking ______
B One possibility is ______
3 A I'm trying to find a way ______
B How ______

a. getting an English-speaking tutor.
b. to understand English recipes.
c. in learning English for travel.
d. about taking a cooking class in English?
e. for a way to improve my pronunciation.
f. getting an English travel magazine

Lesson C Brainstorm!

Make a list of ways to communicate and ways to avoid communicating. You have two minutes.

Lesson D Find out!

Who are two people both you and your partner send instant messages to – or would like to send messages to? You and your partner have one minute.

A: *I send instant messages to my mom. Do you?*

B: *No, I don't. She doesn't use messaging apps. I send instant messages to my sister. Do you?*

A: *Yes, I do.*

2 In the real world

How did your grandparents use to communicate with their friends and family? Talk to one of your grandparents or an older friend. How did they communicate before there were computers and cell phones? Write about it.

How My Grandparents Used to Communicate

My grandmother talked to her friends on a phone in her house. She also wrote them letters.

3 Food

LESSON A

- Food preparation
- Present passive

LESSON B

- Giving a recommendation
- Accepting a recommendation

LESSON C

- Tastes and textures
- Time clauses

LESSON D

- Reading: "What Will You Be Eating 25 Years from Today?"
- Writing: A recipe

Warm Up

A Describe the pictures. What foods do you see?

B What have the foods been made into?

A Street food

1 Vocabulary Food preparation

A Match the words and the pictures. Then listen and check your answers.

a	bake	c	fry	e	melt	g	roast
b	boil	d	grill	f	microwave	h	steam

1 ☐
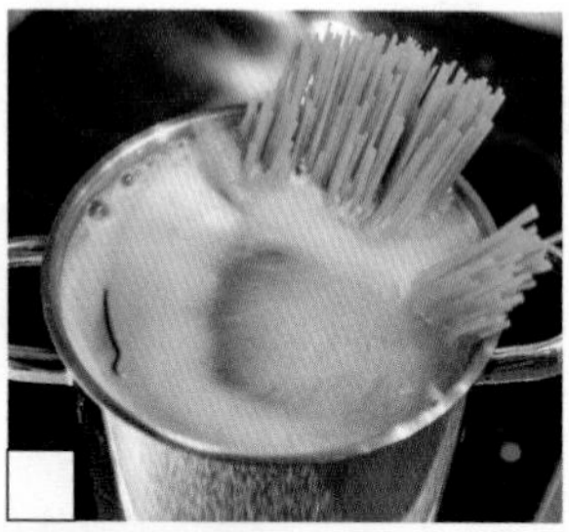
2 ☐

3 ☐
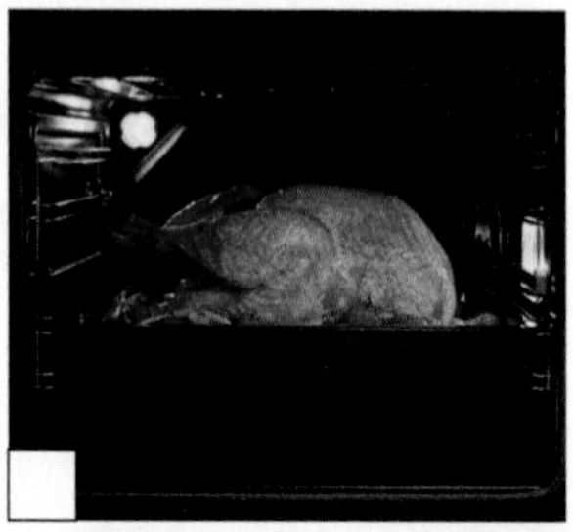
4 ☐

5 ☐

6 ☐

7 ☐

8 ☐

B PAIR WORK **What food can you prepare with each method in Part A? What food can't you prepare with each method? Tell your partner.**

"You can melt cheese, but you can't melt fish."

2 Language in context On every street corner

A Read the descriptions of popular street foods. What ingredients are mentioned?

Empanadas are a typical street snack in the Dominican Republic. They're dough that is filled with meat, vegetables, cheese, or a combination of all three. Then they're fried.

Bagels are a kind of bread that is sold by street vendors all over New York City. Bagels are boiled and then baked. They're often eaten with butter or cream cheese.

Satay is very popular in Indonesia. There are many types of satay, but usually meat is put on wooden sticks and then grilled. Satay is often served with peanut sauce.

B What about you? Do you have similar foods where you live? Which would you like to try right now?

3 Grammar Present passive

The active voice places the focus of a sentence on the doer of an action. The passive voice places the focus on the receiver of the action. Use the passive voice when the doer is not known or is not important.

Active	Passive
You **serve** satay with peanut sauce.	Satay **is served** with peanut sauce.
The cook **fries** the empanadas	The empanadas **are fried**.
The vendor **boils** and then **bakes** the bagels.	Bagels **are boiled** and then **baked**.

A Complete the sentences with the present passive voice. Then compare with a partner.

1 Tamales are a traditional Mexican food. They ________ (sell) on street corners all over the country. They ________ (make) by filling dough with meat or vegetables. Then the dough ________ (wrap) in corn husks and it ________ (steam).

2 Crepes ________ (eat) as a street snack all over France. Flour, eggs, and milk ________ (mix) together to make a batter. The batter ________ (pour) onto a hot, flat pan, and then it ________ (cook). Crepes ________ (fill) with a variety of ingredients, such as cheese, chocolate, or vegetables.

3 In Japan, *taiyaki* is a popular snack that ________ (shape) like a fish. The sides of a mold ________ (cover) with batter. Then a filling such as sweet red bean paste ________ (add) to the mold. The mold ________ (close), and the taiyaki cakes ________ (cook) until they are golden brown.

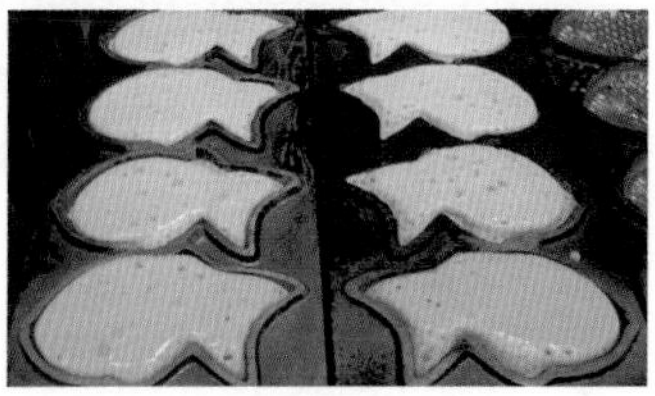

B PAIR WORK **What similarities can you find among the street foods in Exercises 2 and 3? Tell your partner.**

"Both empanadas and crepes are filled."

4 Speaking Popular street foods

GROUP WORK **List three popular street foods. Then discuss these questions for each one.**

- How is it made?
- Where is it sold?
- When is it usually eaten?
- What is it served with?
- How much does it cost?
- What do you like about it?

"Lamb shish kebabs are popular in Turkey. Pieces of lamb are put on a stick and grilled."

5 Keep talking!

Go to page 128 for more practice.

I can describe ways food is prepared.

B Sounds good to me.

1 Interactions Recommendations

A **Do your friends or family ever give you recommendations for good places to eat? Do you ever recommend places to them? What qualities do you look for in a restaurant?**

B **Listen to the conversation. What is each person probably going to order? Then practice the conversation.**

Ralph I'm really glad we could meet for dinner.

Mai So am I. I've been studying so much lately. All I've been eating is junk food.

Ralph I know what you mean. Well, this is one of my favorite restaurants.

Mai Everything looks so good. I have no idea what to get.

Ralph Why don't you try the fish? This place is famous for it. It's grilled and served with fried rice or a baked potato, and a salad.

Mai That's a good idea. Are you going to get the same?

Ralph I'm not sure. I might try the roasted lamb with grilled vegetables.

Mai Oh, that sounds delicious. Will you let me try some?

C **Read the expressions below. Complete each box with a similar expression from the conversation. Then listen and check your answers.**

Giving a recommendation	Accepting a recommendation
______________________	______________________
If I were you, I'd . . .	Sounds good to me.
My recommendation would be to . . .	OK, I think I'll do that.

D PAIR WORK **Have a conversation like the one in Part B. Use these foods.**

2 Pronunciation Linked consonant and vowel sounds

A 🎧 **Listen and repeat. Notice how consonant sounds are often linked to the vowel sounds that follow them.**

if I were you   a good idea   for a long time   rice or potatoes

B 🎧 **Listen to the conversation. Then practice with a partner. Pay attention to the linked sounds.**

A: If I were you, I'd order the steak and shrimp.

B: That's a good idea. Where's our waiter?

3 Listening Eating habits

A 🎧 **Listen to Tom talk to a nutritionist about his eating habits. Write the number of servings of each food Tom eats.**

Food group	Number of servings	Recommendation
Grains (rice, bread, pasta, cereal, etc.)		more / less
Fruits (apples, berries, bananas, etc.)		more / less
Vegetables (lettuce, corn, carrots, etc.)		more / less
Dairy (milk, yogurt, cheese, etc.)		more / less
Protein (meat, fish, eggs, nuts, etc.)		more / less
Fats and oils (butter, olive oil, etc.)		more / less

B 🎧 **Listen again. Does the nutritionist recommend that Tom eat more or less of each food group? Circle your answers.**

4 Speaking Good recommendation!

A **Read the situation. Check (✓) your recommendations and add other ideas.**
My friend has no time to cook. My recommendation would be to ...

- ☐ buy frozen dinners
- ☐ order takeout
- ☐ move back home with parents
- ☐ find a roommate who can cook
- ☐ visit friends at dinnertime
- ☐ other: ____________
- ☐ other: ____________
- ☐ other: ____________

B PAIR WORK **Role-play the situation. Then change roles.**

Student A: You have no time to cook. Listen to Student B's recommendations. Accept one recommendation.

Student B: Student A has no time to cook. Give some recommendations.

A: *I have no time to cook. I don't know what to do.*

B: *If I were you, I'd buy frozen dinners.*

A: *But I don't have a microwave.*

B: *Well, why don't you . . . ?*

I can give and accept recommendations. ✓

C Mix and bake

1 Vocabulary Tastes and textures

A 🎧 **Label the pictures with the correct words. Then listen and check your answers.**

bland	salty	sour	spicy	sweet	chewy	creamy	crunchy	juicy	sticky

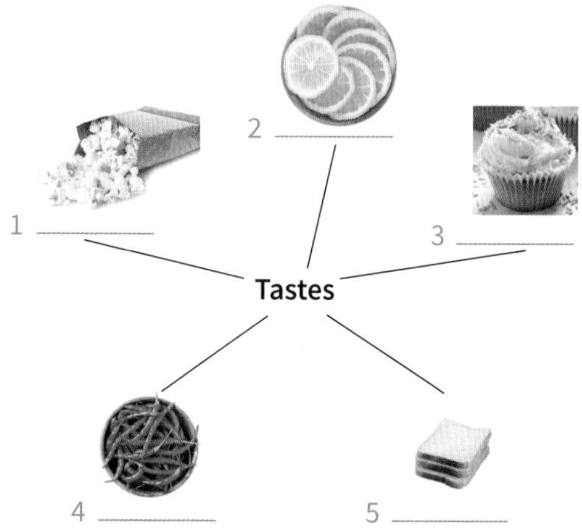

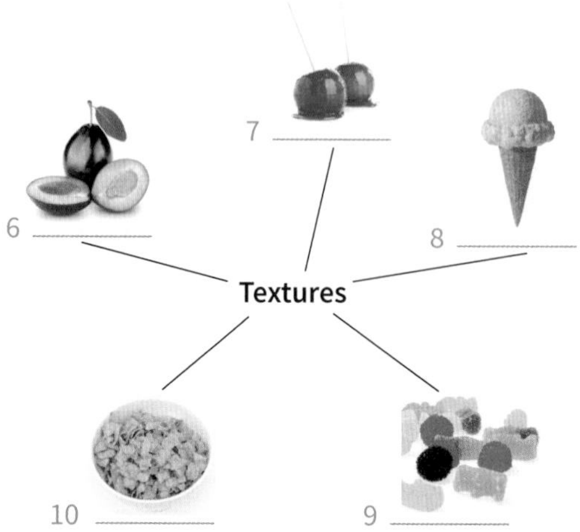

B PAIR WORK **What are some foods that are both salty and crunchy? Sweet and juicy? Spicy and sticky? Sour and chewy? Bland and creamy? Tell your partner.**

"Peanuts are both salty and crunchy."

2 Conversation A guest chef

A 🎧 **Listen to the conversation. What ingredients are in cheese popcorn?**

Host Our guest today is chef Todd Brown. Welcome.

Todd Thank you. Today we're going to make a salty, spicy, and super crunchy snack – cheese popcorn.

Host Sounds good. What do we do first?

Todd Well, we need to make a cheese sauce. But before we do that, we need to make the popcorn. I have some here that I've already microwaved.

Host OK, so after you make the popcorn, you start the cheese sauce. And how do you do that?

Todd Heat some cheese and butter in a pan until they melt. Once the cheese and butter are melted, add some salt and red pepper.

Host Do you need to let the sauce cool?

Todd No. As soon as it's done, pour it over the popcorn. Then bake it for about 20 minutes.

B 🎧 **Listen to the rest of the conversation. What ingredients are in trail mix? How is it described?**

3 Grammar Time clauses

Use time clauses to show the order of events.

Before you start the cheese sauce, you make some popcorn.

After you make the popcorn, you start the cheese sauce.

Heat some cheese and butter in a pan **until they melt**.

Once they're melted, add some salt and red pepper.

As soon as it's done, pour it over the popcorn.

A **Read the recipe. Circle the correct words in the sentences below the recipe. Then compare with a partner.**

PERUVIAN CEVICHE

Ingredients

1 kilogram of fresh fish
8 cloves of garlic
1 chili pepper
juice from 10 limes
salt
1 red onion

Directions

Cut the fish into small pieces. Put them in a bowl.
Chop the garlic and chili pepper. Add them to the fish.
Pour the lime juice in the bowl. This "cooks" the fish.
Add salt. Then mix everything together.
Slice the onion. Place it on top of the mixture.
Let everything sit in the refrigerator for two hours.
Mix and serve immediately with crunchy corn chips.

1. **Before** / **As soon as** you put the fish in a bowl, cut it into small pieces.
2. **Once** / **Until** the fish is in the bowl, chop the garlic and pepper.
3. **Before** / **After** you chop the garlic and pepper, add it to the fish.
4. Add salt **after** / **before** you pour the juice over the mixture.
5. Don't mix the onion with the fish **until** / **once** you remove it from the refrigerator.
6. **As soon as** / **Until** you mix the onion with the fish, serve it and enjoy!

B PAIR WORK **Close your books. Tell your partner the recipe for ceviche.**

4 Speaking A new snack

A PAIR WORK **Use the food in the picture, or other food you know, and create an original snack. Give your snack a name, and describe how to make it.**

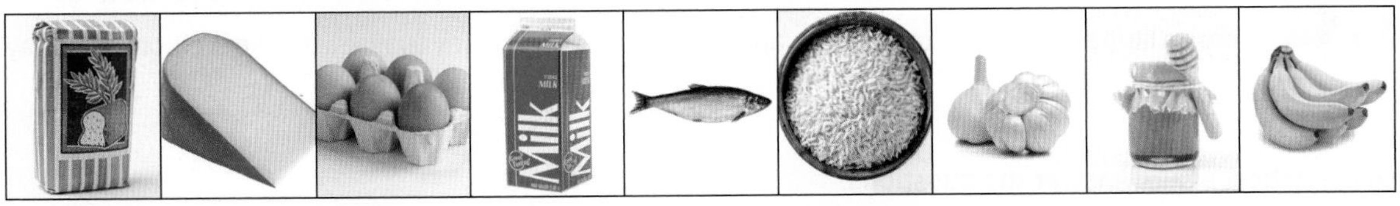

"Here's how to make Spicy Egg Surprise. Boil two eggs until they are done. Once . . ."

B CLASS ACTIVITY **Tell the class how to make your snack. Then vote on the best snack.**

5 Keep talking!

Go to page 129 for more practice.

I can describe steps in a recipe.

D Future food

1 Reading

A What new foods have you tried lately?

B Read the article. Which new foods and technologies are also about sustainability?

What will you be eating 25 years from today?

Long ago, people wouldn't have imagined that you could start your day with a bowl of corn flakes for breakfast, get a sandwich on sliced bread from a drive-through window, or have a bag of potato chips for a snack. That makes us wonder: How will the food we eat and the way we cook be different in 10 or 20 years from now?

Imagine:

You wake up on a Saturday and decide to bake sweet sticky buns for breakfast. You start with a cup of cricket flour – it's a sustainable food made from ground crickets, and it's high in protein. Next you add some honey from the beehive just outside your window – everybody has one now, to help to build the bee population – and bake for 10 minutes.

For lunch, a grilled burger sounds good. Head to your refrigerator and pull out some special meat – it's beef grown in a laboratory rather than in a real cow. If you're a vegetarian, you can get a juicy vegetable burger that is engineered to look, taste, and cook like real beef.

Or if you need to eat on the run, try a liquid supplement with 33 ingredients that has all the protein and other nutrients you need for a balanced meal. Just add water!

For an afternoon snack, grab a handful of crunchy, salty grubs from the worm farm in your kitchen that lets you grow your own super healthy bugs. Or for another nutritious snack, drink a glassful of algae, a tasty green, sustainable treat.

For dinner, roasted chicken sounds good, but you forgot to buy the chicken! No worries – just dip a special fork into a jar of flavored oil, and anything bland that you put in your mouth will smell and taste like roasted chicken.

Finally, for dessert, turn on your 3D food printer and create a delicious, creamy chocolate treat.

Here's a little secret – all of these foods and technologies are already available or in development today!

C Read the article again. Answer the questions.

1. Which dishes are – or could be – vegetarian?
2. Which foods require new technology in your home?
3. Which foods are high in protein?
4. Which foods are sweet?
5. Which foods can you eat on the run?
6. What are the sticky buns made of?

D PAIR WORK What kind of food do you imagine we'll eat in the future? What foods will disappear? What new technology will make it easier to prepare food?

2 Writing A recipe

A Make a list of your favorite dishes. Which dish is the most difficult to make? Which is the easiest?

B Write a simple recipe for one of your favorite dishes. Include the ingredients and the directions.

C PAIR WORK Share your recipe with a partner. Are the steps clear?

Chocolate-covered strawberries

20 strawberries
4–5 chocolate bars chopped nuts
Wash and dry the strawberries.
Boil some water, and then turn off the heat.
Place the chocolate in a bowl over the water.
Stir until it's melted. Remove the bowl from the heat.
Dip each strawberry in the chocolate. Then dip into the nuts.
Put in the refrigerator for 30 minutes.

3 Listening A tour for chocolate lovers

A Listen to Yumiko get information about the San Francisco Gourmet Chocolate Tour. Check (✓) the things that the tour includes.

- ☐ a chocolate factory that makes chocolate bars
- ☐ the winner of *SF Weekly's* "Best Chocolate" Award
- ☐ chocolate that's made using fresh ingredients from local farms
- ☐ a newsstand that sells 225 different kinds of chocolate
- ☐ a sculpture that's made of both white and dark chocolate
- ☐ hot chocolate that's prepared by one of the best chocolate makers in the city
- ☐ a Swiss chocolate maker who is famous for chocolate truffles
- ☐ a Mexican chef who makes a sauce from chocolate and chilies

chocolate truffles

B Listen to the rest of the conversation. Complete the information.

Cost	Meeting place	Times	Group size

4 Speaking A food tour

A PAIR WORK Plan a food tour of a restaurant, a farmers' market, or another place where you live. Answer these questions, and add your own ideas.

- What food will your tour include?
- What places will you visit?
- What will your tour do there?
- Who will lead the tour?
- What will be the cost, meeting place, time, and group size?

A: Everyone likes ice cream. My recommendation would be to create an ice-cream tour.

B: That's a good idea. Or we could do something more unusual. How about a chili-pepper tour?

B CLASS ACTIVITY Share your tour plan. Which tours are the most interesting? Why?

I can discuss what people may eat in the future.

Wrap-up

1 Quick pair review

Lesson A Brainstorm!

Make a list of food-preparation verbs. How many do you know? You have one minute.

Lesson B Find out!

What are two things both you and your partner would eat at a food fair? Give and accept recommendations to find out. You and your partner have two minutes.

A: I want something fried.

B: Me, too. My recommendation would be to try a fried candy bar.

A: That's a good idea.

Lesson C Guess!

Give simple directions for a cooking recipe. Use time clauses. Can your partner guess the food? You and your partner have two minutes.

A: Before you pop it, heat oil in the pan.

B: Is it popcorn?

A: Yes.

Lesson D Give your opinion!

What do you think of these foods? Check (✓) Easy to make or Hard to make. Write a description of the taste and texture. Then discuss. You and your partner have three minutes.

	Easy to make	Hard to make	Taste	Texture
pizza				
lemon cake				
rice				
onion rings				

A: I think pizza is easy to make!

B: I think it's hard to make, but it tastes good. It's spicy and chewy.

2 In the real world

What's your favorite food? Go online or look in a magazine, and find a recipe for it in English. Then write about it.

- What is it?
- What are the ingredients?
- How do you make it?

Chicken and rice

Ingredients: chicken, rice, peanuts, oil, vegetables
Heat the oil. Fry the chicken and vegetables in the oil.
Cook the rice. Put the peanuts on top and serve.

4 Behavior

LESSON A
- Polite and impolite behavior
- Second conditional

LESSON B
- Expressing an expectation
- Acknowledging an expectation

LESSON C
- Word partners
- Past modals for hypothetical situations

LESSON D
- Reading: "Make Someone Happy"
- Writing: An act of kindness

Warm Up

A Look at the picture. Which people are not behaving well?

B Is there behavior at the movies that makes you angry? Would that behavior be OK in a different place?

A The right thing to do

1 Vocabulary Polite and impolite behavior

A Label the phrases P (polite behavior) or I (impolite behavior). Then listen and check your answers.

1 cut in line

2 admit a mistake

3 drop litter

4 talk loudly in public

5 give someone a compliment

6 offer someone your seat

7 keep someone waiting

8 give someone a gift

B PAIR WORK Have you done any of the things in Part A? What happened?

2 Language in context Typical behavior

A Read the survey. Which answer did more than half of the people agree with?

1 What would you do if a stranger dropped litter in front of you?
20% said, "I would talk to the person."
28% said, "I would pick it up."
40% said, "I wouldn't do anything."
12% said, "Other."

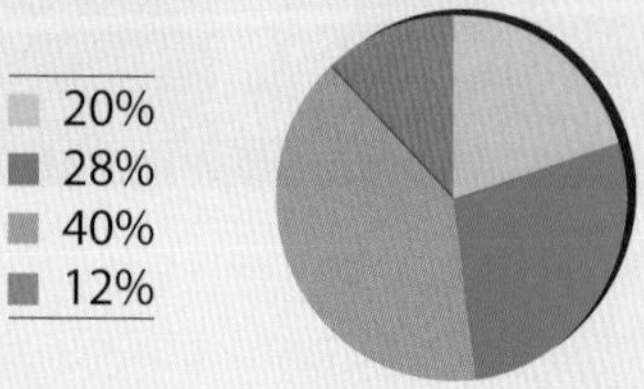

2 If a stranger were talking loudly behind you in a theater, what would you do?
60% said, "I would ask the person to be quiet."
20% said, "I would change seats."
4% said, "I wouldn't do anything."
16% said, "Other."

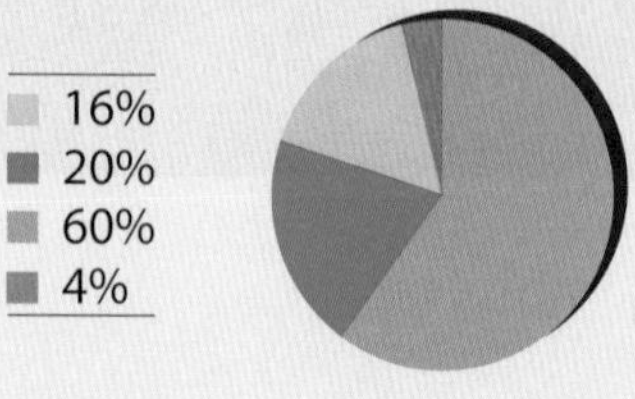

B What about you? Do the responses surprise you? What do you think some of the "other" responses were for each question?

3 Grammar Second conditional

Second conditional sentences describe "unreal" or imaginary situations. Use a past tense verb in the if *clause (the condition). Use* would *in the main clause. Use* were *for the past tense of* be *in the condition.*

If a stranger **were talking** loudly behind you in a movie theater, what **would** you **do**?
I'd change seats. I **wouldn't ask** the person to be quiet.

If a stranger **dropped** litter in front of you, **would** you **pick** it up?
Yes, I **would**. **I'd** probably **throw** it away.

How **would** you **feel** if someone **gave** you a gift for no reason?
If someone **gave** me a gift for no reason, **I'd feel** happy.

A Complete the conversations with the second conditional. Then practice with a partner.

1 A If someone were playing (play) loud music on the subway, what would you do (do)?
B I ______ (ask) the person to turn it down.

2 A What ______ you ______ (do) if a friend ______ (give) you a compliment?
B I ______ (thank) him.

3 A If someone ______ ______ (cut) in line in front of you, what ______ you ______ (say)?
B I ______ (not / say) anything. I ______ (wait) for my turn.

4 A What ______ you ______ (do) if an elderly man ______ (stand) on your bus?
B I ______ (offer) him my seat.

B PAIR WORK **Ask and answer the questions in Part A. Answer with your own information.**

4 Speaking What would you do?

A Complete this question:

"What would you do if ______?"

B CLASS ACTIVITY **Talk to different classmates and ask your question. Take notes on their answers.**

A: What would you do if a friend gave you an unusual gift?

B: I'd probably laugh.

C: I wouldn't do that. I'd smile and say thank you.

C GROUP WORK **Share what you found out. What were the most polite answers?**

5 Keep talking!

Go to page 130 for more practice.

I can discuss how I would react to a situation.

B I didn't realize that.

1 Interactions Expectations

A **Have you ever made a mistake because you didn't know a custom?**

B **Listen to the conversation. What mistake did Ruben make? Then practice the conversation.**

Diana	So, Ruben, how do you like it here?
Ruben	Oh, I love it. The people, the food – but can I ask you something?
Diana	Sure, anything.
Ruben	Well, last night I was invited to a classmate's house for dinner. It was the first time. And I think I made a mistake.
Diana	What happened?
Ruben	Dinner was at 7:30. As usual in my country, I arrived a little after 8:00. My friend seemed kind of surprised.
Diana	Here it's the custom to arrive on time or no more than 10 minutes late.
Ruben	Really? I didn't realize that.
Diana	Well, you'll know for next time.

C **Read the expressions below. Complete each box with a similar expression from the conversation. Then listen and check your answers.**

Expressing an expectation

____

You're supposed to . . .

You're expected to . . .

Acknowledging an expectation

____

Oh, I didn't know that.

Oh, really? I wasn't aware of that.

D **PAIR WORK** **Talk about expectations. Use this information and take turns.**

the United States	Japan	Argentina
Leave a tip of 15 to 20 percent in most restaurants.	Take off your shoes before you enter someone's home.	Begin to eat only after the host or hostess invites you to.
China	**Morocco**	**Russia**
Greet the oldest person in a group first.	Bargain for lower prices on souvenirs in markets.	Bring a small gift if you are invited to someone's home.

A: In the United States, it's the custom to leave a tip of 15 to 20 percent in most restaurants.

B: Oh, really? I wasn't aware of that.

2 Listening Cross-cultural differences

A 🎧 **Listen to four people talk about customs in their country. Write the country name.**

1 ______________________

You're expected to ______________________.

2 ______________________

You're supposed to ______________________.

3 ______________________

It's the custom to ______________________.

4 ______________________

You're not supposed to ______________________.

B 🎧 **Listen again. What is the custom in each country? Write the sentences.**

3 Speaking Good things to know

A **Think about a country you know. Choose three topics below. What are the expectations for polite behavior there? How would you tell a visitor to behave?**

receiving gifts	eating in a restaurant	pointing and gesturing
cutting in line	giving gifts	talking loudly in public
doing business	greeting people	visiting someone's home
dropping litter	money and shopping	walking or driving

B PAIR WORK **Share your ideas.**

A: *In China, you're not supposed to open gifts immediately.*

B: *Really? I didn't know that.*

I can express and acknowledge expectations.

C Doing things differently

1 Vocabulary Word partners

A **Circle the verbs or verb phrases in column A that partner with the nouns in column B. Then listen and check your answers.**

	A	B
1	offer / do / accept	an apology
2	tell / ask for / offer	an explanation
3	agree with / disagree with / turn down	an opinion
4	make / give / turn down	a request
5	deny / give / accept	a compliment
6	admit / ask for / return	a favor
7	reach / say / suggest	a compromise
8	say / accept / turn down	an invitation
9	make / offer / do	an excuse

B PAIR WORK **Ask and answer the question "When was the last time you . . . ?" with four different word partners from Part A.**

A: *When was the last time you asked for a favor?*

B: *Last night. I asked my brother to help me with my homework.*

2 Conversation I feel terrible.

A **Listen to the conversation. Steve asked Paul for a favor. What was it?**

Paul I made a terrible mistake.

Lydia Why? What happened?

Paul Well, you know Steve, the new guy in our class?

Lydia Yeah, I think so.

Paul Well, yesterday he asked me for a favor. He wanted to borrow my laptop. I said I didn't think it was a good idea, and now he's upset with me.

Lydia Really?

Paul Yeah. Should I have lent it to him? What would you have done?

Lydia I'm not really sure.

Paul Well, would *you* have let him use *your* laptop?

Lydia I don't know. I guess it would have depended. What did he need it for?

B **Listen to the phone conversation. Why does Steve call Paul? What does Paul offer Steve?**

3 Grammar Past modals for hypothetical situations

Use past modals to talk about hypothetical situations in the past. Use should have *to talk about the right thing to do,* could have *to talk about possibilities, and* would have *to imagine your behavior.*

I **should have lent** him my laptop.	**Should I have lent** it to him?
I **shouldn't have said** no.	Yes, you **should have**.
He **could have offered** you an explanation.	No, you **shouldn't have**.
It **would have depended**.	What **would** you **have done**?

Complete the conversations with past modals. Then practice with a partner.

1 A My sister loves her new haircut. I told her I hated it. Now she's mad at me.
B That wasn't nice! I wouldn't have said (wouldn't / say) that.
You ______ (could / give) her a compliment instead.

2 A ______ I ______ (should / invite) the whole class to my party? I didn't, and now some people are angry.
B Yes, you ______. But your apartment is really too small.

3 A My cousin asked me for a favor. He wanted to borrow my new car.
What ______ you ______ (would / do)?
B I ______ (would / say) no.

4 A A few days ago, I broke the microwave at my office by accident.
B You ______ (should / offer) to buy a new microwave.

4 Pronunciation Reduction of *have*

A Listen and repeat. Notice how *have* is reduced in past modals.

You could have given her a compliment.
I would have asked her for an explanation.
You shouldn't have said that.
I wouldn't have done that.

B Practice the conversations in Exercise 3. Use the reduced form of *have*.

5 Speaking What would you have done?

A Have you done any of these things? What happened? Choose one and prepare to talk about it.

- You returned a favor.
- You disagreed with an opinion.
- You made an excuse.
- You suggested a compromise.

B GROUP WORK Share your experiences. Would you have done things differently? Discuss your opinions.

A: *Last week, my friend lent me his car. When his car broke down this week, I returned the favor and gave him my car.*

B: *I would have done the same thing.*

6 Keep talking!

Go to page 131 for more practice.

I can talk about past hypothetical situation.

5 Acts of kindness

1 Reading

A Read the quote. What do you think it means?

"No act of kindness, however small, is ever wasted." – Aesop

Make Someone Happy

A man gives a stranger his umbrella during a rainstorm. A teenager picks up litter on her way to school. A woman lets a shopper with fewer groceries cut in line at the supermarket. A man puts money into parking meters on the street so no one gets a ticket.

What do these acts have in common? They are all **random** acts of kindness, **selfless** acts that a person does to make people happy, with nothing expected in return. The acts may be **spontaneous** or planned in advance. The person who receives a random act of kindness may know the person who performed the act, but often the acts are done **anonymously**.

Random acts of kindness are often encouraged by schools and communities. In fact, in some countries, February 17 is Random Acts of Kindness Day, an unofficial holiday. For many people, it's important on this day to "pay it forward." This means if someone does something kind for you, you don't pay "back" that person by returning a kind act to him or her. Instead, you pay it "forward" to someone new. This can be a wonderful way to make both you and someone else very happy.

EXAMPLES OF RANDOM ACTS OF KINDNESS

- Give a stranger a compliment.
- Give someone a gift for no reason.
- Stop and help someone fix a flat tire.
- Let someone cut in line at the bank.
- Offer your seat, and not just to an elderly person.
- Give another driver your parking spot.
- Leave a copy of a good book on a train or a bus.
- Help someone with his or her grocery shopping.
- Offer an apology even if it isn't required.

B Read the article. Find the words in **bold**. Circle the correct meaning.

1	**random**	a. with no pattern	b. with a regular pattern
2	**selfless**	a. putting your own needs first	b. putting others' needs first
3	**spontaneous**	a. with no planning	b. large and important
4	**anonymously**	a. knowing the person's name	b. without knowing the name

C According to the article, which of these would be random acts of kindness? Check (✓) the correct answers.

- ☐ You buy a friend dinner for no reason.
- ☐ You let yourself sleep late on the weekend.
- ☐ You get a job to save money for college.
- ☐ You return a book that you borrowed.
- ☐ You help a neighbor paint his house.
- ☐ You offer your seat to someone

D GROUP WORK Choose an act of kindness from the reading and discuss it. What would you do if someone did it for you? How would you feel? Would you "pay it forward"? How?

2 Listening For no reason

A 🎧 **Listen to four callers to a radio show talk about acts of kindness. Was each act performed or received by them? Check (✓) the correct answer.**

	Performed	Received	Act of kindness
1 Jared	☐	☐	
2 Keisha	☐	☐	
3 Antonio	☐	☐	
4 Mei-li	☐	☐	

B 🎧 **Listen again. What was each act of kindness? Write it in the chart.**

3 Writing An act of kindness

A GROUP WORK **Choose one of these topics. Discuss what happened.**

something nice someone did for you
something nice you did for someone
something nice you'd like to do for someone

B **Write a paragraph about your topic. Use the reading and the model paragraph to help you.**

C CLASS ACTIVITY **Post your paragraphs around the room. Read your classmates' paragraphs. Then get more information about a paragraph that interests you.**

An Act of Kindness

This happened to me last year. I was having a really bad day, so I went to an ice cream shop. I ordered some ice cream, and when I went to pay for it, I couldn't find my wallet. Just then, the person in front of me paid for it! Then she smiled and walked away. I couldn't believe it. She did it just to be nice.

4 Speaking Doing nice things

GROUP WORK **Look at the picture. What would be some nice things to do? Discuss your ideas.**

I can discuss ways to be kind. ✓

Wrap-up

1 Quick pair review

Lesson A Guess!

Think about your partner. How would your partner complete each sentence? Can you guess? Take turns. You and your partner have two minutes.

I ____________________ if I made a mistake.

If someone cut in line in front of me, I ____________________.

I ____________________ if I didn't finish my homework.

A: *You would say you're sorry if you made a mistake.*

B: *No, I wouldn't. I wouldn't tell anyone if I made a mistake.*

Lesson B Do you remember?

Complete the sentences with the correct words to express and acknowledge expectations. You have two minutes.

1 A It's the ____________________ to arrive on time. B Oh, really? I wasn't ____________________ of that.

2 A You're ____________________ to wait in line here. B Oh, I didn't ____________________ that.

3 A You're ____________________ to bring a small gift. B I ____________________ realize that.

Lesson C Test your partner!

Say a verb or a verb phrase that partners with one of the nouns below.Can your partner choose the correct word to make a phrase? Take turns. You and your partner have two minutes.

an apology	a compromise	an explanation	an invitation
a compliment	an excuse	a favor	an opinion

"Ask for."

1 *ask for an explanation* 3 ____________________

2 ____________________ 4 ____________________

Lesson D Find out!

What is one random act of kindness both you and your partner have done? You and your partner have two minutes.

A: *I've given someone my seat on the bus. Have you?*

B: *No, I haven't. I've given my mother a compliment. Have you?*

2 In the real world

What's polite and impolite in different countries? Go online and find three examples of polite and impolite behavior for an English-speaking country. Then write about it.

- What is the country?
- What is the behavior?

Behavior in Australia

In Australia, it's polite to come to meetings on time. It's impolite to miss a doctor's appointment and not call first.

5 Travel and tourism

LESSON A
- Compound adjectives
- Comparatives and superlatives

LESSON B
- Reporting a problem
- Responding to a problem

LESSON C
- Travel talk
- Reporting commands and advice

LESSON D
- Reading: "Welcome to Medellín, Colombia"
- Writing: Creating a home page

1 ☐ Ulan Bator, Mongolia

2 ☐ Wellington,New Zealand

3 ☐ Damascus, Syria

4 ☐ La Paz, Bolivia

5 ☐ Reykjavik,Iceland

6 ☐ Cairo, Egypt

Warm Up

A Look at the capital cities. Match them to their descriptions.

a the coldest	c the oldest	e the highest
b the driest	d the most northern	f the most southern

B What's your capital city like? What three adjectives do you think best describe it?

A Cities

1 Vocabulary Compound adjectives

A Complete the sentences with the correct words. Then listen and check your answers.

culturally diverse
densely populated
fun-loving
high-tech
highly educated
open-minded
slow-paced
well-planned
world-famous

1 Everyone knows New York City. It's a ________________ city with many interesting places to visit.

2 Bangalore is a very ________________ place. It's the center of India's computer industry.

3 For a capital city, Vientiane in Laos is a ________________ place. It's a great place to not be in a hurry.

4 Lagos is a very ________________ city. There are about 20,000 people per square kilometer.

5 Brasília is a ________________ city. There are wide roads, a lot of green space, and great public transportation.

6 Singapore's people are ________________. Many continue their studies after they finish high school.

7 The people in San Francisco are very ________________. They are open to new ideas, opinions, and experiences.

8 There are a lot of ________________ people in San Juan, Puerto Rico. They love to go out and have a good time.

9 London is an extremely ________________ city. You can find people from all over the world there.

B PAIR WORK **Which words in Part A describe people? Which describe places? Which describe people and places? Tell your partner.**

2 Language in context My city

A Listen to three people describe their cities. Where does each person live?

I used to live in Buenos Aires, but I live in Mendoza now. It's not as crowded as Buenos Aires, so it's slower- paced here. But I think the people are pretty fun-loving and open-minded. And there's a great music scene!

– Angela, Argentina

I live in St. Petersburg, but I was born in Moscow. I like both cities, but I prefer St. Petersburg. In the winter, it isn't as cold as Moscow. It's a well-planned city, and I think it's even a little cheaper than Moscow.

– Boris, Russia

I like Osaka for its shopping, but I love it for its food. I think the food is better than in Tokyo. In fact, I think it has the best food in Japan! We have a saying here: "Eat till you drop in Osaka!" I never want to move!

– Nozomi, Japan

B Which city do you think would be good for tourists? Students? Businesspeople? Why?

"Osaka would be good for tourists because the food is good and tourists love to eat!"

3 Grammar Comparatives and superlatives

Comparisons	Superlatives
St. Petersburg is **cheaper than** Moscow.	. . . is **the cheapest** city in Russia.
Buenos Aires is **more crowded than** Mendoza.	. . . is **the most crowded** city.
St. Petersburg is **less expensive than** Moscow.	. . . is **the least expensive** city.
The food in Osaka is **better than** in Tokyo.	. . . is **the best** food in the world.
Traffic here is **worse than** in St. Petersburg.	. . . is **the worst** traffic I've ever seen.

(not) as . . . as	
St. Petersburg isn'**t as cold as** Moscow.	Osaka is **as high-tech as** Tokyo.

A Complete the sentences with the comparative form of the adjectives.

1 Today's high temperature is 29°C in Bangkok and 26°C in Chiang Mai. Bangkok is ______ (hot) Chiang Mai.

2 The average cost of a new house in Tokyo is around 35 million yen. The average cost of a new house in Kinki is around 29 million yen. New houses in Tokyo are ______ (expensive) houses in Kinki.

3 There are 7,200 people per square kilometer in São Paulo, and 5,200 people per square kilometer in Rio de Janeiro. São Paulo is ______ (densely populated) Rio.

4 Mumbai usually gets 87 centimeters of rain and very little sunshine in July. In January, there is almost no rain, and the weather is mild and sunny. The weather in July is ______ (bad) in January.

B PAIR WORK **Say each sentence in Part A in a different way. Use *not as . . . as*.**

"Chiang Mai isn't as hot as Bangkok."

C Complete the questions with the superlative form of the adjectives. Work with a partner. Ask and answer with your own information.

1 What's the most high-tech (high-tech) city in your country?

2 What's ______ (bad) restaurant in your town?

3 What's ______ (culturally diverse) city in your country?

4 What's ______ (less populated) part of your country?

4 Speaking Comparing three cities

GROUP WORK **Compare three cities you know. Talk about:**

education	food	shopping	transportation
entertainment	people	traffic	weather

A: Why don't we compare Curitiba, São Paulo, and Belo Horizonte? OK.

B: São Paulo is bigger than Curitiba.

C: Curitiba is the most well-planned of the three.

5 Keep talking!

Go to page 132 for more practice.

I can make comparisons about cities.

B I'll let someone know.

1 Interactions

A What do you think are the most common hotel complaints? If you had a problem with a hotel room, what would you do?

B Listen to the conversation. What's the problem? Then practice the conversation.

Clerk Front desk. Please hold.

. . . .

Clerk Thank you for waiting. How can I help you?

Lina Um, hi. I just checked in a few minutes ago. There's a problem with my Internet connection. I can't get a wireless signal.

Clerk I'm very sorry. I'll let someone know right away.

Lina Thank you. I'd appreciate it.

Clerk Is there anything else I can help you with?

Lina Um, yeah. Can you recommend a restaurant near the hotel?

Clerk Yes, there are several, but our hotel restaurant is one of the best in the city.

C Read the expressions below. Complete each box with a similar expression from the conversation. Then listen and check your answers.

Reporting a problem	Responding to a problem
______________________	______________________
I'm having a problem with . . .	I'll get someone to take care of it.
There seems to be a problem with . . .	I'll have someone get on it right away.

D PAIR WORK Have conversations like the one in Part B. Use these problems.

The air-conditioning isn't working.

The table lamp doesn't have a bulb.

The bathroom sink is clogged.

The door has a broken knob.

2 Pronunciation Linking of same consonant sounds

Listen and repeat. Notice the linking of the same consonant sounds at the end and beginning of words. The sound is pronounced only once.

There's no wireless signal.

The radio has a broken knob.

The bathroom mirror is dirty.

The table lamp doesn't have a bulb.

3 Listening How can I help you?

A Listen to three people call the front desk at a hotel. Check (✓) the problem.

	Problem	Response	Solved?
1	☐ She hears a strange noise. ☐ She can't close her windows.		yes no
2	☐ The TV won't turn on. ☐ There's no battery in the remote.		yes no
3	☐ There isn't any electricity. ☐ The desk lamp needs a new bulb.		yes no

B Listen again. How does the man at the front desk respond to the problems? What does he say he will do? Write the sentences in the chart.

C Listen. A hotel worker comes to solve each problem. Does he? Circle yes or no.

4 Speaking Problems, problems, problems

PAIR WORK **Role-play the situation. Then change roles.**

Student A: Call the front desk three times to report three problems in your hotel room.

Student B: You work at the front desk. Answer the phone and respond to each problem.

A: *There's a problem with my room. There are bugs on the wall.*

B: *I'll have someone get on it right away.*

I can report and respond to a problem.

C Travel experiences

1 Vocabulary Travel talk

A Read Luke's travel blog. Complete the chart with the bold words in the blog. Then listen and check your answers.

LUKE'S TRAVEL BLOG

Sunday, August 25th

My trip's been full of surprises so far. First, my flight here was **delayed**. I took the next one, and I was **upgraded** to first class! Then I discovered that my visa was **expired**, but I was **issued** one at the airport on arrival. Good thing! But they lost my luggage.

When I went to my two-star hotel, I found out it was **overbooked**. But I had a reservation, and it was **guaranteed**. So, they put me in a four-star hotel for the same price.

I read that the museums here are always **packed** and the restaurants are **overrated** and **overpriced**. But I went to a museum early this morning, and there were only a few people there. I even got a **discounted** ticket! After that, I went to a famous restaurant for lunch. It was priced right, and it was the best meal I've ever had.

Good experiences

1 ____________
2 ____________
3 ____________
4 ____________

Bad experiences

5 ____________
6 ____________
7 ____________
8 ____________
9 ____________
10 ____________

B What experiences have you had like Luke's? Which have you never had?

2 Conversation Welcome home!

A Listen and practice. Where's Luke's luggage?

Jae-Sun Luke! Welcome home!
Luke Hi, Jae-Sun. Thanks for picking me up.
Jae-Sun That's what friends are for. I read your blog. I can't believe your flight was delayed and your hotel was overbooked.
Luke I know, but things turned out OK.
Jae-Sun Hey, where's your luggage?
Luke They never found it! The man at the airport told me to be patient.
Jae-Sun Patient? Are you serious? You've *been* patient.
Luke Well, he advised me to call in a few days to check on it. Anyway, look! I got you a souvenir.
Jae-Sun Really? Thank you!

B Listen to a phone conversation between Luke and the man at the airport. Where is Luke's luggage now? When can he expect his luggage?

3 Grammar Reporting commands and advice

These reporting verbs are followed by an object + infinitive. Notice the placement of not.

The man said:

"Be patient."	He **told me to be** patient.
"Don't be impatient."	He **told me not to be** impatient.
"Remember to take your room key."	He **reminded us to take** our room key.
"Don't forget your room key."	He **reminded us not to forget** our room key.
"Call in a few days."	He **advised me to call** in a few days.
"Don't carry a lot of cash."	He **warned her not to carry** a lot of cash.

Look at your friend Maria's travel advice. Rewrite her advice. Use reporting verbs. Then compare with a partner.

1	"Get a good guidebook."	tell	*She told me to get a good guidebook.*
2	"Don't pack too much."	tell	
3	"Buy a youth hostel card."	advise	
4	"Get a visa."	remind	
5	"Don't go out at night alone."	warn	
6	"Keep your passport safe."	tell	
7	"Use ATMs to get cash."	advise	
8	"Don't forget to write."	remind	

4 Speaking Good advice

A CLASS ACTIVITY **Talk to different classmates. What advice would they give an overseas visitor to their city? Write their names and advice in the chart.**

Advice about . . .	Name	Advice
a tourist attraction to avoid	*Diego*	*Don't go to street fairs. They're packed and overrated.*
a "must-see" tourist attraction		
a restaurant to avoid		
the best way to get around		
a good way to save money		

B GROUP WORK **Imagine you are the overseas visitor. Report the advice you heard. Does everyone agree with the advice?**

"Diego advised me not to go to street fairs. They're packed and overrated."

5 Keep talking!

Go to page 133 for more practice.

I can report commands and advice.

D My town, the best town

1 Reading

A Do you like to visit new places? What things do you especially like to see and do?

B Read the headings under *Travel essentials* and *Things to see and do*. What topics are covered under *Travel essentials*? What topics are covered under *Things to see and do*?

Welcome to Medellín, Colombia the City of Everlasting Spring

TRAVEL ESSENTIALS

Climate

Medellín is located at about 5,000 feet (1,538 meters) above sea level. Its climate is not as hot as other cities located near the equator. The city's average temperature is a pleasant 72°F (22°C). Read more

Getting here

Medellín has an international airport, with flights from Miami, New York, Madrid, and many other cities. There are taxis and minibuses from the airport to downtown Medellín. Read more

Getting around

The quickest and cheapest way to get around Medellín is with the well-planned metro and tram system. The modern Turibus also goes around the city, showing parks, beautiful neighborhoods, and historical sites. Read more

Where to stay

There are many hotels, but hostels are also popular, especially when hotels are overbooked. Many hostels include hot showers, TV, laundry service, free Wi-Fi, private lockers, and Spanish lessons. Read more

THINGS TO SEE AND DO

Nightlife

The fun-loving people of Medellín love to dance. There are many places around the city to dance. One of the most famous is the Zona Rosa. Most clubs close at 3:00 a.m. Read more

Sightseeing

There are world-famous museums in the city, but one "must-see" is the Museo de Antioquia. It has a large collection of art, including paintings and sculptures by Fernando Botero. Read more

Festivals

Why not plan a trip around a festival? There's a poetry festival in July, a celebration of lights in December and January, and for two weeks in August, a flower festival – the city's most important cultural event. Read more

Day trip

Located just two hours from the city is the town of Guatapé where you can see the most wonderful views from the top of La Piedra, or The Rock. It has an elevation of about 7,000 feet (2,135 meters) above sea level, and 740 steps were built to reach the top. Read more

C Read the home page. Answer the questions.

1 How can you get from the airport to downtown? __________
2 What's the least expensive way to get around the city? __________
3 Where can you enjoy a fantastic view? __________
4 What's one of the most famous places to go to at night? __________
5 What can you find at the Museo de Antioquia? __________
6 When is the flower festival? __________

D Imagine you had only one day in Medellín. How would you spend your day?

2 Writing Creating a home page

A GROUP WORK What kind of information might appear on your town's home page? Make a list of topics. Use the topics in Exercise 1 to help you.

B GROUP WORK Create and design a home page for your town. Have each student write a paragraph about a topic from your list in Part A. Use Exercise 1 and the model to help you.

> **Shopping**
> *Our town is a shopper's paradise! There is something for everyone, and the prices are great. You can buy textiles, jewelry, and the painted wooden creatures that so many tourists love. . . .*

C CLASS ACTIVITY Post your home pages around the room. Which home page best represents your town?

3 Listening City festivals

A Listen to four people talk about city festivals. Complete the second and third columns of the chart.

	Name of the festival	Year started	Month of the festival	One thing to see or do
1	Milan Melon Festival			
2	Pusan International Film Festival			
3	Historic Center Festival Of Mexico City			
4	Edinburgh Festival Fringe			

B Listen again. Complete the chart. Write one thing to see or do at each festival.

C Which festival would you most like to attend? Why?

4 Speaking A festival to remember

A GROUP WORK Plan a festival for your town. Use these ideas or ideas of your own for fun events at the festival.

a contest	a parade
a fashion show	a sporting event

A: *Our town is well known for corn.*
B: *So why don't we have a Corn Festival?*
C: *We could have a corn-eating contest.*

B CLASS ACTIVITY Share your ideas.

I can discuss ideas for a festival in my town.

Wrap-up

1 Quick pair review

Lesson A **Do you remember?**

Match the words. You have one minute.

1	fun- ______________	a.	tech
2	open- ______________	b.	minded
3	densely ______________	c.	paced
4	high- ______________	d.	loving
5	highly ______________	e.	educated
6	well- ______________	f.	populated
7	Culturally ______________	g.	diverse
8	slow- ______________	h.	famous
9	world- ______________	i.	planned

Lesson B **Brainstorm!**

Make a list of ways to report a problem and respond to a problem. How many do you know? You have two minutes.

Lesson C **Test your partner!**

Give your friend travel advice using commands. Can your partner say the sentence using reported commands or advice? Take turns. You and your partner have one minute.

A: *Make a reservation.*

B: *You told me to make a reservation.*

Lesson D **Find out!**

How would you and your partner answer these questions? You and your partner have two minutes.

- What's the most expensive restaurant in your town?
- What's the best festival in your country?
- What's the most high-tech building in your town?

A: *I think the most expensive restaurant is Sushi King.*

B: *Me, too!*

2 In the real world

What country would you like to visit? What two cities in that country would you like to see? Find information online or in a travel magazine about these cities. Then write about them.

- Which city is more densely populated?
- Which city is slower-paced?
- Which city is cheaper?
- Which city has better weather?

Two Cities in Peru

I'd like to visit Lima and Arequipa in Peru. Lima is more densely populated than Arequipa.

6 The way we are

LESSON A
- Character traits
- Defining relative clauses

LESSON B
- Interrupting politely
- Agreeing to an interruption

LESSON C
- Tips to manage stress
- *Wish*

LESSON D
- Reading: "Therapies That Work!"
- Writing: About relaxation

Pizza and you

Crust: You are very adventurous. You love to try new things.

Sauce: You like trendy things. You enjoy the finer things in life.

Cheese: You don't care for trendy things. You prefer tradition.

Spices: You enjoy traditional and modern things equally.

Meat: You are strong and like to be in control of any situation.

Other toppings: You make changes easily. You like everyone and everything.

Source: Adapted from www.blogthings.com/whatsyourpizzapersonalityquiz

Warm Up

A Look at the picture. What is your favorite part of a pizza? Check (✓) the box.

B Read the *Pizza and you* box. What does your answer in Part A show about your personality? Do you agree? Do you think personality tests like this can tell you about your personality?

A Who I am

1 Vocabulary Character traits

A **Match the adjectives and the descriptions. Then listen and check your answers.**

1 competitive ______
2 energetic ______
3 idealistic ______
4 imaginative ______
5 independent ______
6 logical ______
7 loyal ______
8 rebellious ______
9 studious ______

a. You believe you can make good things happen.
b. You want to be better than everyone else.
c. You are active and enthusiastic.
d. You think and act without help from others.
e. You make decisions based on facts.
f. You always think of new and creative ideas.
g. You spend time studying and learning new things.
h. You do not follow other people's rules.
i. You always support people and places you know.

B PAIR WORK **Describe people you know with these traits. How do they show these traits?**

"My friend is very idealistic. She says she wants to make the world a better place, so she volunteers a lot."

2 Language in context Personality types

A **Read these personality types. Which personality type best describes someone who studies all the time? likes to have fun? makes decisions quickly?**

1 The **Reformer** is logical and idealistic. This type of person wants everything to be perfect.
2 The **Helper** is caring and generous. This type likes to please people.
3 The **Achiever** is a person who wants success. This type of person is studious and ambitious.
4 The **Individualist** is sensitive and often quiet. This type likes to be independent.
5 The **Investigator** is curious and creative. This is a person who is always questioning things.
6 The **Loyalist** is hardworking, responsible, and extremely loyal. This is someone that people can trust.
7 The **Enthusiast** is optimistic and spontaneous. This type of person is cheerful and fun-loving.
8 The **Challenger** makes decisions that other people find difficult to make. This type is confident and powerful.
9 The **Peacemaker** dislikes situations which create conflict. This type is easygoing and agreeable.

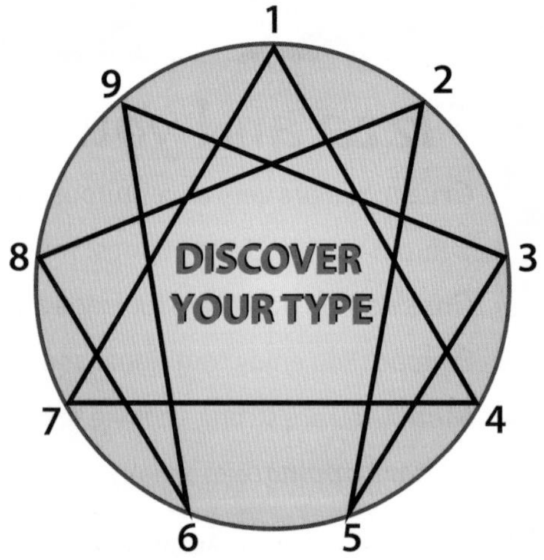

Source: Adapted from www.enneagraminstitute.com

B **What about you? What personality type are you?**

3 Grammar Defining relative clauses

Defining relative clauses supply essential information about a noun. They answer the questions "what kind" or "which one(s)." Use the pronouns who *or* that *for people. Use* which *or* that *for things.*

The Achiever is a person **who / that wants success.**

The Peacemaker dislikes situations **which / that create conflict.**

The relative pronouns are optional when they are the object of the relative clause.

The Loyalist is someone **(who / that) people can trust.**

The Challenger makes decisions **(which / that) other people find difficult to make.**

A Complete the sentences with *who or which.*

1 My sister has a rebellious side ________ my parents never see.
2 I like friends ________ are easygoing and loyal.
3 I hardly ever do things ________ are spontaneous.
4 I have idealistic views ________ some people can't understand.
5 I was a studious child ________ was also very energetic.
6 My brother is a person ________ other people find competitive.

B Cross out *who*, *which*, or *that* when it's optional.

1 I'm the kind of person ~~that~~ other people think is very logical about things.
2 I can make decisions that others find difficult to make.
3 Do you think you have any personality traits which people dislike?
4 What would be a good job for someone who is independent and responsible?

C PAIR WORK Compare your answers in Parts A and B. Then complete these sentences with your own information.

I like people who . . .

I like to do things which . . .

I'm someone that other people . . .

4 Speaking Personality and jobs

A PAIR WORK Look at the personality types in Exercise 2. Which personality type(s) would be good for these jobs?

a businessperson   a musician   a police officer   a politician   a teacher

B GROUP WORK What kind of job do you think would be good for you? What are your character traits that would help you succeed?

"I'm a person who likes to be independent. I'd be good at a job that lets me work at home."

5 Keep talking!

Go to page 136 for more practice.

I can talk about character traits.

B Sorry, but can I ask something?

1 Interactions Interruptions

A **Do you ever interrupt friends who are talking? What do you say to interrupt them? When is it OK to interrupt someone, and when is it impolite?**

B **Listen to the conversation. Why does Carol interrupt Kevin?**

Kevin	Did you see that? I can't believe he's safe!
Carol	What a great play! He's one of the most competitive players I've ever seen. Why do you think some people are so competitive?
Kevin	Well, maybe he's the middle child.
Carol	What do you mean?
Kevin	People who have an older and younger brother or sister are often very competitive. I just read something about that. And people who –
Carol	Sorry, but can I ask something?
Kevin	Sure. Go ahead.
Carol	Where did you read that? That's crazy.
Kevin	In a psychology magazine. I can show you. Anyway, as I was saying . . . the youngest person in the family is often the most outgoing and confident.
Carol	That's me! Maybe it's not so crazy.

C **Read the expressions below. Complete each box with a similar expression from the conversation. Then listen and check your answers.**

Interrupting politely

____

I'm sorry, but could I ask one thing?

Before you go on, could I ask something?

Agreeing to an interruption

____

Yeah, of course.

OK. Sure.

D PAIR WORK **Number the sentences from 1 to 6. Then practice with a partner.**

_____ A What about friends?

__1__ A Do you think a husband and wife should have similar personalities?

_____ A Well, before you go on, could I ask something else?

_____ B I think it's different with friends. But husbands and wives have to have some interests in common.

_____ B Similar personalities? No, it's better to be different. But I also think . . .

_____ B OK. Sure.

2 Pronunciation Stress in thought groups

A **Listen and repeat. Notice how long sentences are divided into shorter thought groups. The most important word in each thought group receives stronger stress.**

Why do you **think** / **some** people / are so **competitive**?

B **Listen. Mark the stressed word in each thought group. Then practice with a partner.**

1 Before you go on / could I ask something?

2 And the youngest person / in the family / is often / very outgoing / and confident.

3 Listening Type A and Type B personalities

A **Listen to Emily give a presentation on Type A and Type B personalities. How many times do her classmates interrupt?**

B **Listen again. How does Emily describe each personality type? Check (✓) the words.**

Type A		Type B	
☐ independent	☐ impatient	☐ easygoing	☐ imaginative
☐ hardworking	☐ energetic	☐ patient	☐ relaxed
☐ ambitious	☐ competitive	☐ logical	☐ idealistic

C **Do you know someone who has a Type A personality? Do you know someone who has a Type B personality? How are they different? How are they the same?**

4 Speaking Opinions on personality

A **Choose a topic and take notes to prepare for a discussion.**

Topic	Notes
1 Three qualities of a great friend	
2 Three good character traits	
3 Three reasons people are competitive	

B GROUP WORK **Begin a discussion on your topic. Interrupt one another politely to add to the discussion.**

A: *A great friend is someone who is loyal and always ready to help.*

B: *Before you go on, could I ask something?*

I can interrupt politely.

I can agree to an interruption.

C Wishing for change

1 Vocabulary Tips to manage stress

A Match the phrases and the pictures. Then listen and check your answers.

a balance work and play	c find time to relax	e live within a budget
b be more organized	d lead a healthier lifestyle	f manage time better

1 ☐

2 ☐

3 ☐

4 ☐

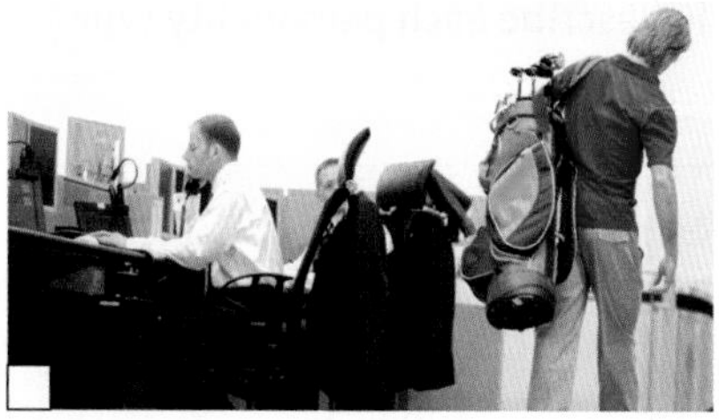
5 ☐

6 ☐

B PAIR WORK Which tips in Part A would help you? Why?

"I want to balance work and play. I work all the time. I don't have time to relax."

2 Conversation Stressed out

A Listen to the conversation. Why is Rosa stressed out?

Rosa How was your weekend?

Jules Great. I saw a movie, finished a great novel, and went out with friends.

Rosa Where do you find time to relax like that? I wish I had more free time.

Jules What's keeping you so busy?

Rosa Work and school, mostly. I wish there were more hours in the day.

Jules Listen, I have this book. It's about ways to manage stress. It has great tips on managing your time better.

Rosa Like what?

Jules Well, for example, it recommends making a plan of what you want to achieve each day.

Rosa I wish I could read it now, but it's not part of my plan! I don't have the time.

B Listen to the rest of the conversation. What causes Jules stress? What is he doing about it?

3 Grammar *Wish*

Use wish + *a past tense verb to talk about present wishes. For wishes with the verb* be, *use* were *with both singular and plural nouns and pronouns.*

I **have to** study.	→	I wish I **didn't have to** study.
I **don't have** enough free time.	→	I wish I **had** more free time.
I **can't** read it now.	→	I wish I **could** read it now.
I **am** so busy.	→	I wish I **weren't** so busy.
I **am not** very organized.	→	I wish I **were** more organized.

A Complete the sentences with the past form of the verbs.

1 I wish I ______________ (not / worry) so much.
2 I wish I ______________ (can find) more time to relax.
3 I wish I ______________ (do) better in school.
4 I wish my schedule ______________ (not / be) so full.
5 I wish I ______________ (not / have) to do chores every day.
6 I wish my brother ______________ (can visit) me this week.

B Write sentences with *wish* and the phrases in the box.

balance work and play	be more organized	lead a healthier lifestyle
be more easygoing	be more studious	manage time better

1 I'm always late for everything. ______________
2 I get stressed over little things. ______________
3 I don't get enough exercise. ______________
4 I'm not an organized person. ______________
5 I have trouble concentrating on my studies. ______________
6 I can't find time to relax. ______________

C PAIR WORK Compare your sentences in Parts A and B. Which sentences are true for you?

4 Speaking Make a wish.

A Do you wish you could change any of these things? Write down three wishes.

my friends and family	my possessions
my personality	my school or job
my clothes	my skills and abilities

B GROUP WORK Share your wishes.

A: *I wish I had a car.*
B: *Me, too! I wish I could get a sports car.*
C: *I wish I had a driver's license!*

5 Keep talking!

Go to pages 134–135 for more practice.

I can talk about present wishes.

D Alternative therapies

1 Reading

A Are alternative therapies popular where you live? Have you ever tried one?

B Read the article. Which of these therapies are used in hospitals?

THERAPIES THAT WORK!

Aromatherapy helps calm stress with pleasant smells. Some smells relax people. Others make people more energetic. Popular scents include fruit, grasses, and flowers. In Japan, engineers have created aroma systems in public buildings. They send different scents into the air to create a better environment. For example, customers who are waiting in long lines at some banks might smell fresh flowers to help them relax.

Pet therapy uses animals to help calm and comfort people, especially young patients in hospitals and older people in nursing homes. The animals are brought to the hospitals and homes so that patients can see and touch them. This has an amazingly relaxing effect. Pet therapists usually use dogs and cats, but sometimes rabbits, birds, horses, and even llamas are used.

Color therapy uses colors to change your mood and emotions. Color therapists believe that the colors around you can affect you in different ways. For example, the color blue can relieve pain, and the colors red and orange can make you energetic. Some therapists even believe different parts of the body are influenced by different colors. They believe that having the right colors around you can help you get better when you are sick.

Humor therapy helps you find ways to laugh or smile. Laughter reduces stress and fear and anger. Many hospitals encourage their nurses to laugh with their patients, or put funny pictures on the walls. In India there are "laughing clubs" where people come together in the morning to tell funny stories, just to have a good laugh to start the day. Laughter is often the best medicine.

C Read the article again. What therapies are pictured? Number the pictures from 1 to 4 in the order you read about them.

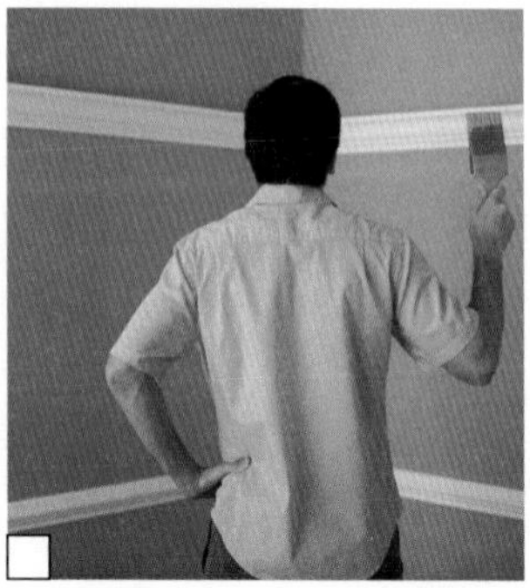

D What do you think of the therapies? Would you like to try any of them? Do you think they work? Do you think they could be harmful in any way?

2 Listening Guided imagery

A 🎧 **Listen to a therapist discuss guided imagery. What is guided imagery? Check (✓) the answer.**

☐ a way to see new things ☐ a way to reduce stress ☐ a way to practice aromatherapy

B 🎧 **Listen again. Check (✓) the true sentences.**

1 ☐ Guided imagery uses your imagination.
2 ☐ One of the best things to use it for is to reduce pain.
3 ☐ You can only use the technique with a therapist.
4 ☐ It's important to be in a comfortable place.
5 ☐ Some people think it can help you learn.

C 🎧 **Listen to an exercise in guided imagery, just for fun. Follow the directions. How do you feel after listening?**

3 Writing About relaxation

A **What do you do to relax? Write about it. Use the questions and the model paragraph to help you.**

- What techniques have you tried to help you relax?
- What worked?
- What didn't work?
- What do you wish you could try to help you relax?

Relaxing

My job is very stressful, so when I have some free time, I try to do things to help me relax. I've tried yoga and baking. Yoga really helps me relax my body and my mind, and I do it twice a week. Baking didn't work for me because I made a big mess in the kitchen, so I got more stressed because of that. I wish I could . . .

B PAIR WORK **Share your writing. Do you do similar things to relax?**

4 Speaking Relaxing creatively

A GROUP WORK **Look at the ways that some people relax. Which do you think would work for you? Which wouldn't? Why not?**

keeping a pet	painting
baking	shopping
cleaning the house	singing in the shower
dancing	watching a horror movie
keeping a journal	watching the stars
watching fish	writing poetry
listening to rock music	yelling alone in a forest

A: *I think playing with a dog would help me relax.*
B: *Me, too. But writing poetry wouldn't. That would be stressful for me.*

B CLASS ACTIVITY **Brainstorm other creative ways to relax. Share them with the class.**

I can discuss ways to relax. ✓

Wrap-up

1 Quick pair review

Lesson A **Find out!**

Which two family members do both you and your partner have with these character traits? You and your partner have two minutes.

- A family member who is competitive
- A family member that's very loyal
- A family member who is idealistic and imaginative

A: *I have a brother who is competitive. Do you?*

B: *No, but my aunt is competitive.*

A: *So is my aunt!*

Lesson B **Do you remember?**

Check (✓) the expressions that show interrupting politely. You have one minute.

1 ☐ Sorry, but can I ask something?

2 ☐ Oh, really? I'm not sure about that.

3 ☐ Sure. Go ahead.

4 ☐ I'm sorry, but could I ask one thing?

5 ☐ Before you go on, could I ask something?

6 ☐ I'll let someone know right away.

Lesson C **Guess!**

Tell your friend about a problem. Can your partner guess what you wish? Take turns. You and your partner have two minutes.

A: *I have a lot of homework. I have three meetings this week. I have to call my mother.*

B: *You wish you weren't so busy.*

Lesson D **Give your opinion!**

What things do you and your partner think cause stress? What things do you think reduce stress? Write them in the chart and compare. You have two minutes.

Things that cause stress	Things that reduce stress

2 In the real world

Which therapy are you interested in? Who does it help? Go online and find information about one of these therapies. Then write about it.

- adventure therapy
- art therapy
- light therapy
- writing therapy

Light Therapy

Light therapy uses light to make you feel better. It is for people who live in places that don't get a lot of sunlight. They use bright lamps in their homes

7 New ways of thinking

LESSON A
- Positive and negative descriptions
- *So* and *such*

LESSON B
- Eliciting an idea
- Suggesting a solution

LESSON C
- Verb and noun formation
- The passive

LESSON D
- Reading: "Technology Helps Japan's Elderly"
- Writing: An invention

Warm Up

A Look at the pictures. What do you see?

B What problem did each of these creations try to solve? Do you think they were successful?

A Inventions

1 Vocabulary Positive and negative descriptions

A **Make the words negative. Write them in the chart. Then listen and check your answers.**

convenient	creative	eventful	significant
conventional	effective	imaginative	successful

un-	in-

B PAIR WORK **What do you think? Discuss the sentences. Circle the correct word.**

1. The first computers were huge. They filled an entire room. They were very **convenient** / **inconvenient** for everyday use.
2. Coco Chanel's fashion designs are world famous. They were so **imaginative** / **unimaginative**. Many people have copied them.
3. The new hybrid car is **conventional** / **unconventional**. I've never seen one like it. It uses air, not gasoline.
4. One day in 1847, Joseph Fry discovered a way to make chocolate bars. What an **eventful** / **uneventful** day that was! What would we do without them?

2 Language in context Early inventions

A **Read the descriptions of early inventions. What was each invention used for?**

The abacus is over 5,000 years old. It was used to count numbers. It was such an effective tool in China and the Middle East that it spread to other parts of the world and is still used in many countries today.

Rubber was first used by the ancient Mayans in Mexico and Central America about 3,500 years ago. They took rubber from trees, boiled it, and made rubber balls, which they used in ancient ball games.

More than 2,000 years ago, the ancient Romans built aqueducts to bring water into their cities from miles away. Some of these aqueducts were so well made that they still carry water today.

B **What are some modern examples of these inventions? Do you know any other early inventions?**

3 Grammar So and *such*

Use so *and* such *with an adjective to make the adjective*

so + adjective	such + a / an + adjective + singular noun
It was **so creative**.	It was **such a creative** idea.
It was **so well made**.	It was **such a well-made** aqueduct.

Use a that *clause with* so *or* such *to show a result.*

The abacus was **so** effective **that** it spread to other places.

The abacus was **such** an effective tool **that** it spread to other places.

A Complete the sentences with *so* or *such*. Then compare with a partner.

1. The wheel was ______ a significant invention.
2. Her ideas were ______ unimaginative.
3. His inventions have been ______ successful.
4. His thinking is ______ unconventional.
5. She was ______ a creative woman.
6. Wireless Internet access is ______ convenient.

B Complete the sentences. Use *so . . . that* or *such . . . that*. Then compare with a partner.

1. Online streaming is ______ (popular) cable TV subscriptions have decreased.
2. I think the Perfect Cake Cutter was ______ (an ineffective invention) no one wanted to buy it.
3. Smartphones are ______ (inexpensive) almost everyone has one.
4. MP3 players were ______ (a big success) they changed the way we listen to music.

4 Pronunciation Emphatic stress

A Listen and repeat. Notice the extra stress on *so* and *such* for emphasis.

That is **so** conventional. That is **such** a conventional thing to say.

B PAIR WORK Practice the sentences in Exercise 3A. Pay attention to your pronunciation of *so* and *such*.

5 Speaking Top inventions

GROUP WORK Discuss three important inventions in each category. Why are they so important?

communication	technology	transportation

6 Keep talking!

Go to page 137 for more practice.

I can describe important inventions.

B Got any suggestions?

1 Interactions Solutions

A **Look at the picture in Part B. What problem do the people have? How can they solve it?**

B **Listen to the conversation. How do they plan to solve the problem? Then practice the conversation.**

Ralph	Here we go . . . almost there.
Carl	This sofa is going to look great in my living room. Thanks again for helping me.
Jim	No problem.
Ralph	Wait a minute. It doesn't fit.
Carl	What? Are you kidding?
Jim	Did you measure it before you bought it?
Carl	Of course. There should be enough room. I even made a sketch, see?
Ralph	Well, I'm sure there's something we can do. Do you have any ideas?
Jim	Well, one idea could be to turn the sofa the other way.
Carl	It's worth a try. If that doesn't work, I'm not sure what else to do.

C **Read the expressions below. Complete each box with a similar expression from the conversation. Then listen and check your answers.**

Eliciting an idea

____

Got any ideas?

Got any suggestions?

Suggesting a solution

____

Something we could try is to . . .

One solution might be to . . .

D **GROUP WORK** **Have conversations like the one in Part B. Use these ideas.**

go through the window

remove the legs

2 Listening Sticky situations

A **Look at the pictures. What problems do you see?**

☐ 

☐ 

☐ 

☐ 

B **Listen to people discuss how to solve the problems in Part A. Number the pictures in Part A from 1 to 4.**

C **Listen again. Check (✓) the solution they decide to try.**

1 ☐ Stand on the reef and lift the boat.
☐ Wait and let the tide lift the boat.

2 ☐ Take the parrot's cage outside.
☐ Give the parrot treats.

3 ☐ Pour oil around the opening.
☐ Put the jar under hot running water.

4 ☐ Add weight to push the truck down.
☐ Remove all the air from the tires.

3 Speaking Inventive solutions

A **GROUP WORK** **What could you do in these situations? Discuss your answers.**

1 You forgot your wallet and have no money to pay for the dinner you have just eaten at a restaurant.

2 Your pet cat is sitting at the end of a high tree branch. It's so scared that it won't come down.

3 You realize you made plans with your best friend and your mother for the same night.

4 You discover you locked your keys inside your apartment.

A: *Do you have any ideas about situation 1?*

B: *Well, one idea could be to call a friend for help.*

C: *Or one solution might be to wash the dishes to pay for your meal.*

B **CLASS ACTIVITY** **Share your solutions. Vote on the best solution for each situation.**

I can elicit ideas. ✓

I can suggest solutions. ✓

C Accidental inventions

1 Vocabulary Verb and noun formation

A **Read about the inventions. Complete the chart with the missing form of words. Then listen and check your answers.**

Sometimes a successful **invention** happens by accident: the tea bag, for example. Thomas Sullivan **introduced** tea bags to the world in 1908. He was a New York tea importer. He sent tea to his clients in tin cans. But tin was so heavy and expensive that he needed a more convenient way to send it. So he **designed** inexpensive bags to hold the tea leaves and sent them instead. Thomas's customers were supposed to open the bags and put the leaves in hot water. Instead, they used the entire bag. But this **innovation** worked! Immediately, tea bags **proved** to be a big **success**.

Ruth Wakefield **created** another accidental invention in her Massachusetts hotel in 1930. One day, Ruth didn't have enough chocolate for her usual chocolate cookie recipe. So she cut a chocolate bar into small pieces and made more cookies with less chocolate. The chocolate chips didn't melt completely, but her guests loved them! Ruth **developed** the original chocolate chip cookie. And her recipe has never needed much **improvement**. It's still the world's most popular chocolate chip cookie recipe today.

Verb	Noun
invented	*invention*
	introduction
	design

Verb	Noun
innovated	
	proof
succeeded	

Verb	Noun
	creation
	development
improved	

B **PAIR WORK** **Choose four of the words from the chart. Make sentences with these words about something you have done. Tell your partner.**

2 Conversation A delicious discovery

A **Listen to the conversation. Why did the chef get angry?**

Dana Do you know how the potato chip was invented?

Emma I have no idea.

Dana Apparently, in 1853, a customer in a restaurant sent his French fries back to the kitchen several times because they weren't thin enough. The chef was so angry that he sliced them even thinner, fried them again, and sent them back to the customer.

Emma And the customer liked them?

Dana Yeah, he asked for more! The chef's creation was such a success that they were requested by other customers, too. At that time they were only salted, but since then, lots of different flavors have been developed.

Emma Fascinating. So, can I have my chips back?

B **Listen to the rest of the conversation. What three countries do they mention? What flavors of potato chips are mentioned for each country?**

3 Grammar The passive

Active		Passive
Simple present:	People still **use** her recipe today.	Her recipe **is** still **used** today.
Simple past:	A chef **invented** it in 1853.	It **was invented** in 1853.
Present perfect:	Companies **have developed** many flavors since 1853.	Many flavors **have been developed** since 1853.

A Rewrite these sentences. Use the passive voice. Then compare with a partner.

1 Thomas Sullivan introduced tea bags to the world in 1908.
Tea bags were introduced to the world in 1908.

2 Sullivan designed small bags to hold the tea.
______

3 A man produced the first flavored potato chip in the 1950s.
______

4 Potato chip makers have developed many unique flavors.
______

B Complete the sentences. Use the passive voice with the simple present, simple past, or present perfect form. Then compare with a partner.

The 3M company ______ (know) for its innovation for a long time. But there have been mistakes along the way. Today, employees ______ (encourage) to learn from past mistakes. That's how Arthur Fry learned about a special glue. It ______ (create) in the 3M lab in 1968. The glue wasn't strong enough, so it ______ (forget). But Fry found it in 1974 and used it to develop Post-it Notes. The original Post-it Notes ______ (improve) since then, and now they ______ (sell) all over the world.

4 Speaking Early innovations

GROUP WORK Look at these products. What improvements have been made to the products recently? Have all of the improvements been good ones?

"Tennis shoes have been made lighter. Their design has been improved a lot."

5 Keep talking!

Go to page 138 for more practice.

I can discuss how things have been improved.

D Making life easier

1 Reading

A Look at the picture. What do you think this article is about?

B Read the article. Check (✓) the best title.

- ☐ Top Innovations in Japan
- ☐ Technology Helps Japan's Elderly
- ☐ The Future of Technology
- ☐ Growing Old in Japan

ONCE UPON A TIME,

there was a land where robotic bears helped lift the elderly out of bed and into wheelchairs. In this land, robotic seals comforted lonely people and were an **essential** part of elder care.

Is this science fiction? Not in Japan. These robots already exist, and you may actually experience them as you get older. These examples of **state-of-the-art** technology are helping to solve a big problem for the Japanese – the problem of taking care of their **senior citizens**.

It is estimated that 40% of the population in Japan will be over 65 by 2055. At the same time, there will be an estimated 16% decrease in the size of the workforce by 2030. This **shortage** of labor presents a serious challenge:

Who will look after all the people in their **golden years**? There are simply not enough younger people to care for this older population. And with the breakdown of traditional family responsibilities, a growing number of elderly are living away from their families and the family care they have been given in the past.

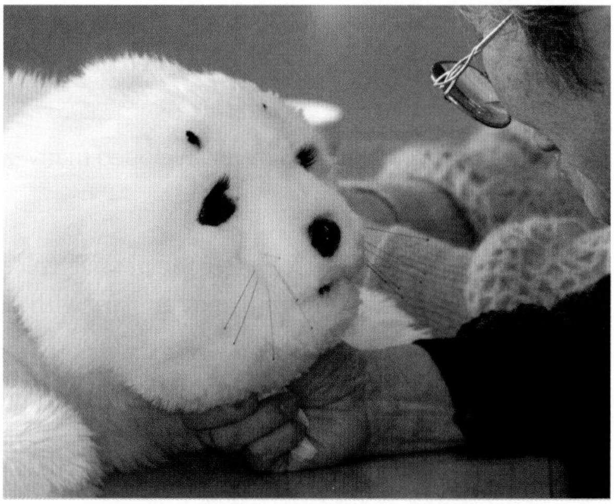

Robots to the rescue! Robotic beds that are controlled by voice can change from a bed to a wheelchair on command. The robotic bear nurse can lift patients who weigh up to 135 pounds (61 kilos). And for comfort and friendship, a soft robotic pet seal has been designed to show emotions with facial expressions, movement, and noises, and to respond to touch. These are just a few of the inventions that are so promising. Robots are the future of elder care.

C Find the words in **bold** in the article. Circle the correct meanings.

1	**essential**	a. necessary	b. unnatural
2	**state-of-the-art**	a. the most advanced	b. imaginary
3	**senior citizens**	a. elderly people	b. people who need help
4	**shortage**	a. too much of	b. not enough of
5	**golden years**	a. time before retirement	b. time after retirement

D CLASS ACTIVITY What is your opinion of using robots and technology to help the elderly? What are some other ways that robots and technology are helping people? Discuss your ideas.

2 Listening A robot pet?

A Listen to a commercial for i-Cybie, a robot dog. Check (✓) the things the i-Cybie can do.

- [ ] eat
- [ ] sing
- [ ] play
- [ ] sit
- [ ] scratch its ear
- [ ] dance
- [ ] taste
- [ ] smell
- [ ] show emotion
- [ ] sleep
- [ ] respond to commands
- [ ] do a yoga position

B Listen to Jason tell his friend Tina about his new i-Cybie. Write two things he likes and two things he doesn't like about his new pet.

What he likes	What he doesn't like
1 ______	1 ______
2 ______	2 ______

3 Writing and speaking An invention

A GROUP WORK **Brainstorm inventions that would make your life easier. Make a list.**

B **Choose one of the inventions. Draw a picture of it. Then write a paragraph about it. Give it a name, explain who it's for, and discuss what it does.**

Charger Baseball Cap
The Charger Baseball Cap is for anyone who loves laying out in the sun, but doesn't want to worry about their phone battery. The front of the cap has a solar charging panel that wirelessly charges your cell phone. It looks like a stylish baseball cap, but . . .

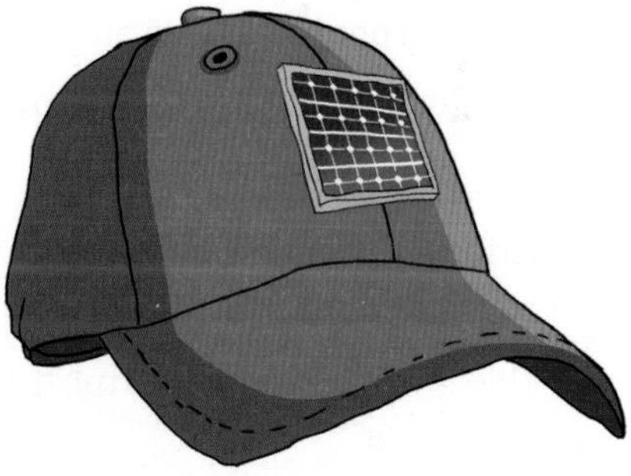

C CLASS ACTIVITY **Walk around the class. Show the picture of your invention to five people. Describe it and try to convince your classmates that they need your invention.**

"You have to get a Charger Baseball Cap. You can charge your phone battery while you're outside, but you also . . ."

D **As a class, vote on and give these awards for the best inventions.**

the best overall invention	the most innovative invention
the greatest improvement to people's lives	the most useful invention

I can describe something I invented.

Wrap-up

1 Quick pair review

Lesson A Test your partner!

Say a positive descriptive adjective. Can your partner write the negative adjective correctly? Take turns. You and your partner have one minute.

"Conventional."

1 *unconventional* 3 ______ 5 ______

2 ______ 4 ______ 6 ______

Lesson B Give your opinion!

What are solutions to these problems? Elicit ideas and suggest solutions. Take turns. You and your partner have two minutes.

- You have only one day to study for a test.
- You can't find your keys.
- You have a broken-down car and need to get to work.
- You have to fit a big piano through a small door.

A: *I have only one day to study for a test. Got any suggestions?*

B: *One idea could be to stay up all night and study.*

Lesson C Do you remember?

Write A for active and P for passive. You have one minute.

1 The Internet was invented in the 1970s. ______

2 My mother doesn't like new technology. ______

3 This cell phone has won an award for best design. ______

4 That movie has been seen all over the world. ______

Lesson D Guess!

Describe an invention, but don't say its name. Can your partner guess what it is? You and your partner have two minutes.

A: *This invention is so useful. It helps you see.*

B: *Glasses?*

A: *No. It goes in a lamp.*

2 In the real world

What's a great invention? Find information online about one of these inventions, or choose your own idea. Then write about it.

computer mouse	pencil sharpener	Silly Putty	TV remote control

- What is it?
- Who invented it?
- When was it invented?
- What do you think about the invention?

Silly Putty

Silly Putty is a toy for children. It was invented by James Wright in the 1940s.

8 Lessons in life

LESSON A
- Prefixes: *mis-*, *dis-*, and *re-*
- Past perfect

LESSON B
- Expressing worry
- Reassuring someone

LESSON C
- Expressions with *make* and *get*
- Third conditional

LESSON D
- Reading: "Tuesday, January 9, 2007"
- Writing: About a memorable day

Warm Up

A Describe the pictures. What's happening? How do you think each person feels?

B What would you do if these things happened to you?

A Why did I do that?

1 Vocabulary Prefixes: *mis-*, *dis-*, and *re-*

A **Read the sentences. Match the prefixes *mis-*, *dis-*, and *re-* and their meanings.**

1 I **mis**spelled your name. Can you correct it? ____ a. do something again

2 Please **dis**regard my email. It wasn't important. ____ b. do something wrong

3 Let's **re**consider. There might be a better way. ____ c. don't do something

B **Add the correct prefixes to the words, and write them in the chart. Then listen and check your answers.**

agree	continue	judge	make	regard	think
consider	do	like	pronounce	spell	understand

mis-	dis-	re-
____ ____	____ ____	____ ____
____ ____	____ ____	____ ____

C PAIR WORK **Answer the questions.**

- What word do you often misspell? What word do you often mispronounce?
- Do you ever disagree with your friends? Do you disregard their advice? Why?

2 Language in context Awkward situations

A **Listen to two people describe awkward situations. What was awkward about each situation?**

When I was emailing my classmate about a surprise party for my friend Leo, I hit "send" and it went to Leo. I'd sent the email to Leo before I realized my mistake. I called him and asked him to disregard the email. Luckily, he hadn't read it yet.

– John

The other day, my boss mispronounced my name in the elevator. He had done it once before, and I hadn't corrected him. But this time, I reconsidered. Unfortunately, by the time I started to say something, my boss had already left the elevator.

– Angelica

B **What do you think? Did John and Angelica do the right thing? Has anything similar ever happened to you?**

3 Grammar Past perfect

Use the past perfect to describe an action that took place before another action in the past.

I'd sent the email to Leo before I realized my mistake.

The words yet and already are often used with the past perfect.

I asked him to disregard the message. Luckily, **he hadn't** read it yet.

By the time I started to say something, my boss **had** already **left**.

Contraction *I'd = I **had***

Complete the sentences. Use the simple past and past perfect in each sentence. Then compare with a partner.

1 I ____________ (plan) on working all weekend, but then I ____________ (reconsider) and went to the beach instead.

2 I was so late this morning. By the time I ____________ (get) to work, I ____________ (miss) the whole meeting.

3 Alice ____________ (wake up) at 9:30 because she ____________ (forget) to set her alarm clock for 8:00.

4 Before Richard and Alex ____________ (meet), they ____________ (be) e-pals for a year.

5 I ____________ (call) my friend to cancel our plans. Luckily, he ____________ (not / leave) yet.

4 Pronunciation Reduction of *had*

A Listen and repeat. Notice how *had* is pronounced /d/ in the past perfect.

I'**d** sent the email to Leo. My boss **had** already left the elevator.

B PAIR WORK Practice the sentences in Exercise 3. Pay attention to your pronunciation of the past perfect.

5 Speaking I'd forgotten to . . .

A Choose a situation and prepare to talk about it. Think about the events that happened *before* and *after*.

you disagreed with someone	you misjudged someone	you redid something incorrectly
you forgot something	you misunderstood someone	you were very late

B GROUP WORK Tell your classmates what happened. Answer any questions.

A: *I was embarrassed at a job interview once. I'd forgotten to turn off my cell phone.*

B: *Really? Did the job interviewer say anything?*

6 Keep talking!

Go to page 139 for more practice.

I can describe events in the past.

B I'm sure you'll do fine.

1 Interactions Worries and reassurance

A In which of these situations do you feel the most confident? The least confident?

public speaking in English	speaking in front of a large group
public speaking in your own language	speaking in front of a small group

B Listen to the conversation. What is Feng worried about? Then practice the conversation.

Mei Hi, Feng. How are you?

Feng Oh, hi, Mei. I'm fine, I guess. But I have to give a presentation in my English class, and I'm kind of worried about it.

Mei Really? Why?

Feng Well, I always forget what I'm planning to say. I'm not confident speaking in front of people.

Mei Can you use notes?

Feng Yeah, I can, so that will help.

Mei I'm sure you'll do fine. You're great in front of people.

Feng Do you really think so?

Mei I do. Just try to relax.

Feng Well, thanks. We'll see how it goes.

C Read the expressions below. Complete each box with a similar expression from the conversation. Then listen and check your answers.

Expressing worry

____

I'm a little anxious about it.

I'm pretty nervous about it.

Reassuring someone

____

I'm sure you'll be OK.

Don't worry. Everything will work out.

D PAIR WORK Number the sentences from 1 to 6. Then practice with a partner.

_____ A When is it?

__1__ A Hi, Bill. How are you?

_____ A This weekend? Well, I'm sure you'll do OK.

_____ B Really? I'm not so sure. But thanks anyway.

_____ B It's this weekend.

_____ B Fine, I guess. But I'm pretty nervous about my driver's test.

2 Listening Feeling anxious

A 🎧 **Listen to four friends talk about situations that worry them. Number the pictures from 1 to 4.**

B 🎧 **Listen again. What do their friends say to reassure them? Write the sentences.**

1 ____________________

2 ____________________

3 ____________________

4 ____________________

3 Speaking Please don't worry.

A PAIR WORK **Role-play the situation.**

Student A: You have been invited to a party. You are a little anxious about it. You're afraid you won't know anyone. Tell Student B how you feel.

Student B: Student A is a little anxious about going to a party. Find out why. Reassure your friend.

A: *I'm pretty nervous about going to this party.*

B: *Why are you so nervous?*

A: *I won't know anyone there.*

B: *But you can meet new people there. Don't worry. . . .*

B **Change roles and role-play the situation.**

Student A: You are changing schools. You are worried about it. You're afraid you might not make new friends easily. Tell Student B how you feel.

Student B: Student A is changing schools and is worried about it. Find out why. Reassure your friend.

C PAIR WORK **Write a role play about reassuring someone in a difficult situation. Give it to another pair to role-play. Use one of these situations, or use your own ideas.**

doing a home-stay abroad	getting a new roommate	traveling alone

I can express worry. ✓

I can reassure someone. ✓

C What if...?

1 Vocabulary Expressions with *make* and *get*

A Match the statements. Then listen and check your answers.

1 I hate to **make a fool of myself.** ______
2 I always **make an effort** to do my best in school. ______
3 I often **make mistakes.** ______
4 I never **make a big deal** about my birthday. ______
5 I **make up my mind** easily. ______
6 I never **get into trouble.** ______
7 If someone isn't nice to me, I try to **get over it** quickly. ______
8 I always try to **get out of** doing the dishes. ______
9 My friends sometimes **get on my nerves.** ______
10 I like to **get rid of** things I don't need. ______

a. I sometimes don't even tell anyone.
b. I dislike it when people laugh at my mistakes.
c. I try very hard.
d. I am careless.
e. It's not difficult for me to decide things.
f. I just disregard it.
g. I always try to follow the rules.
h. I get annoyed when they play loud music.
i. It's my least favorite chore.
j. I don't like to keep unnecessary things.

B PAIR WORK **Which statements in Part A are true for you? Discuss your answers.**

"I like to get rid of old newspapers and magazines, but my roommate likes to save them."

2 Conversation A new boyfriend

A Listen to the conversation. What mistake did Alicia make?

Dan: So, how was Aki's party?
Alicia: Well, the party was fun. But I'd forgotten it was her birthday, so I was a little embarrassed.
Dan: Why?
Alicia: I didn't bring a gift. If I'd remembered, I'd have brought her something really nice.
Dan: Well, I'm sure she didn't mind.
Alicia: Then, I think I made a fool of myself at the party. We all had to sing, and you know how bad my voice is.
Dan: Oh, come on.
Alicia: I tried to get out of it, but I couldn't. And that's when I met Santiago. Just think. If I hadn't sung at the party, I wouldn't have met Santiago.
Dan: Santiago? Who's Santiago?
Alicia: He's my new boyfriend.

B Listen to the rest of the conversation. What's Santiago like? What gets on Alicia's nerves?

3 Grammar Third conditional

Third conditional sentences describe hypothetical situations in the past.
Use the past perfect in the if *clause and would* have + *past participle in the main clause.*
If I'**d remembered**, I **would have brought** her something.
If I **hadn't forgotten**, I **would have brought** her a gift.
If she **had missed** the party, she **wouldn't have met** Santiago.
If she **hadn't gone** to the party, she **wouldn't have met** him.
Remember: I'**d** = I **would** *or* I **had**

A Read the conditional sentences. Circle the true statements about them.

1 If Henry had made an effort, he would have passed all of his exams.
a. Henry made an effort. b. Henry didn't make an effort.

2 If Mike had followed the instructions, he wouldn't have made a mistake.
a. Mike made a mistake. b. Mike didn't make a mistake.

3 If Luz hadn't become a doctor, she would have become an artist.
a. Luz became a doctor. b. Luz didn't become a doctor.

4 If Andrea hadn't sold her old books online, she wouldn't have gotten rid of them.
a. Andrea got rid of her books. b. Andrea didn't get rid of her books.

B Complete the sentences with the third conditional. Then compare with a partner.

1 If I __________ (know) about the party,
I __________ (not / make) such a fool of myself.

2 If you __________ (come) home before midnight,
you __________ (not / get) into trouble.

3 If I __________ (not / get) rid of my old cell phone,
I __________ (let) you have it.

4 I __________ (make) up my mind easily if
I __________ (not / have) so many choices.

4 Speaking If only I hadn't . . .

A Check (✓) the things you've done.

☐ made a mistake
☐ made an effort to do something
☐ made a fool of yourself
☐ gotten rid of something important
☐ gotten out of something
☐ gotten into trouble

B PAIR WORK **Tell your partner the things you checked in Part A. What would have been different if you hadn't done these things? Share your stories.**

5 Keep talking!

Go to page 140 for more practice.

I can talk about how things might have been.

D A day to remember

1 Reading

A **The great hockey player Wayne Gretzky once said: "I skate to where the puck is going to be, not where it has been." Why do you think Steve Jobs liked this quote so much?**

Tuesday, January 9, 2007

STEVE JOBS

co-Founder and CEO of Apple, was about to walk onto a stage in San Francisco. Moments before, he had gathered his team together and told them to remember this moment, because in the next hour, everything would change.

Jobs was about to unveil the iPhone, which would become one of the most popular products of all time.

The team was more than a little nervous about the event. When they had arrived that day, the iPhone didn't actually work yet. It would often crash when trying to play a song or run an app. But the company had been working to remake the mobile phone for 2 ½ years, and Jobs made up his mind it was time to introduce the iPhone to the world. The engineers had prepared a presentation with features they thought could work, but they were terrified they might have made some mistakes.

It wasn't the first time that Apple had launched a revolutionary product. When Apple introduced the Macintosh computer in 1984, it changed personal computing forever. And when the company launched the first iPod music player in 2001, it revolutionized the way we listen to music – and the way music is sold.

Despite the pressure, Jobs was calm. He was used to speaking in front of a large group. After he had taken the stage, he told the crowd he actually had three revolutionary new products to show them – a touchscreen iPod, a mobile phone, and an Internet device. "Are you getting it?" he asked. "This is one device. And we are calling it iPhone."

If the presentation had failed, it would have been a disaster. But everything went perfectly. Jobs showed the crowd of 4,000 how you could easily switch from surfing the Internet to making a call to listening to music. He demonstrated how you could use your fingers to zoom in on a photo, and how Apple had gotten rid of the physical keyboard with buttons that was common on other phones. And he showed how the iPhone put the Internet in your pocket for the first time, letting you check your email or surf the Web from anywhere.

A number of other products had included some of these features, but the iPhone was the first to combine them all – and a lot more. When Jobs had finished his presentation, mobile phones would never be the same again.

B **Read the excerpt again. Number the events from 1 to 8.**

_____ Jobs told his team to remember this moment.
_____ Jobs took the stage.
_____ The Apple team prepared a presentation.
_____ Jobs made up his mind to unveil the iPhone.
_____ Jobs demonstrated the iPhone's features.
_____ Apple launched the iPod.
_____ The Apple team developed the iPhone.
__1__ Apple introduced the Mac computer.

C **Do you remember a time before the iPhone? What do you imagine that mobile phones were like at that time? How do you think people surfed the Internet, took pictures, listened to music, and followed maps before the iPhone?**

2 Listening Looking back

A Listen to four people talk about important days in their lives. Check (✓) which day they're talking about.

	Day	What made it a memorable day?
1	☐ first day of middle school ☐ first day of high school	☐ Her friend was a teacher at the school. ☐ Her friend was going to the same school.
2	☐ wedding day ☐ birth of a child	☐ Their parents were there. ☐ The announcement appeared in the newspaper.
3	☐ first day at work ☐ last day at work	☐ His co-workers gave him a party. ☐ He'd traveled on his own in Europe.
4	☐ first airplane trip ☐ first trip over seas	☐ She could speak Korean with her host family. ☐ Her hosts were so kind and friendly.

B Listen again. Check (✓) what made the day memorable.

3 Writing and speaking About a memorable day

A Think about a memorable day. Use these ideas or your own ideas.

the day you got accepted to college	your first airplane ride
the day you spoke English to a native speaker	your first day at a new job
the first time you rode a bicycle	your first day of school
a special celebration	

B Write a paragraph about your memorable day. Use the questions and the model paragraph to help you.

- When was it?
- What made the day memorable?
- Did you look forward to this day?
- What did you do that day?
- How did you feel then?

A Memorable Day

One of the best days of my life was when I got accepted to City University. I had always wanted to go there. I'd been pretty worried until I got my official acceptance letter. I remember I called some of my friends to tell them. Then that night, I went out with my family to celebrate. I was so happy that day.

C GROUP WORK Share your writing. Ask and answer questions about that day. As a group, decide which day was the most interesting, unusual, or exciting day.

I can describe a memorable day. ✓

Wrap-up

1 Quick pair review

Lesson A Do you remember?

Cross out the words that don't belong. You have one minute.

1	*mis-*	spell	understand	~~think~~	pronounce	judge
2	*re-*	do	think	consider	make	agree
3	*dis-*	agree	make	continue	regard	like

Lesson B Brainstorm!

Make a list of ways to express worry and ways to reassure someone. How many do you remember? You have two minutes.

Lesson C Give your opinion!

Imagine these things happened to you. Ask your partner what he or she would have done. Take turns. You and your partner have two minutes.

- You forgot to take your passport to the airport.
- You didn't remember a friend's birthday.
- You didn't go to class on the day of a test.

A: What would you have done if you had forgotten your passport?

B: If I had forgotten my passport, I would have called my friend and asked her to bring it to me. What about you?

Lesson D Guess!

Think about important first days in a person's life. Guess how old your partner was for each of these firsts. You and your partner have two minutes.

first time he or she traveled alone	first time he or she spoke English
first time he or she rode a bicycle	(your own idea)

A: Were you 18 the first time you traveled alone?

B: No, I was younger.

2 In the real world

What was the first day of school like for someone in your family or for a close friend? Interview the person. Then write about it.

First Day of School

My father was nervous on his first day of school. His father, my grandfather, took him to school. My father met Charlie on the first day of school. Charlie became his best friend.

9 Can you believe it?

LESSON A
- Suffixes: *-ful* and *-less*
- Past modals for speculating

LESSON B
- Expressing probability
- Expressing improbability

LESSON C
- Mysterious events
- Embedded questions

LESSON D
- Reading: "The Woman Who Can't Forget"
- Writing: A story

Warm Up

A Describe the pictures. What do you see?

B Can you explain the pictures? Think of several possible explanations.

A Everyday explanations

1 Vocabulary Suffixes: *-ful* and *-less*

A Circle the correct words to complete the sentences. Then listen and check your answers.

1 I can't get this old computer to work at all. It's **useful** / **useless** for me to even try.
2 The storm was so **powerful** / **powerless** that it destroyed a hundred homes.
3 I read about a man who raised a lion as his pet. He was totally **fearful** / **fearless**.
4 The police made people leave the building because the bad odor was **harmful** / **harmless** to their health.
5 Jane was fined $300 for **careful** / **careless** driving.
6 I couldn't understand his explanations at all. They were so **meaningful** / **meaningless**.
7 Sara gave me a lovely graduation present. That was very **thoughtful** / **thoughtless** of her.
8 I'm **hopeful** / **hopeless** that I'll get a good grade on my exam. I have been studying a lot.

B PAIR WORK Make sentences about your experiences. Use the words you did *not* circle in Part A. Tell your partner.

2 Language in context Explainable behavior

A Read the online chat between co-workers. Why are they talking about Kenny?

Online Chat

Maria, Ethan, James...

Maria: Ethan, did you see Kenny yesterday?

Ethan: How could I miss him? He was wearing a suit. He looked so impressive in his suit and tie! ☺.

Maria: Yeah, I know. But it was really hot yesterday, so he couldn't have been comfortable in a suit.

Ethan: Did you ask him why he was so dressed up?

Maria: Yeah, but it was useless. He wouldn't say a word.

Ethan: He might have had a presentation to give.

Maria: Yeah, that's possible. Or maybe it wasn't meaningful at all. He could have simply felt like dressing up in a suit.

James: Hi, you guys. Did you hear about Kenny?

Ethan: Actually, we were just chatting about him.

James: Well, he called me earlier today. He said he had interviewed for a new job yesterday. And they offered it to him!

Maria: That explains it! He must have gone to his interview after work. He wasn't very careful about it, was he?

Write a Message... Send

B What are some other reasons that people dress up for work?

3 Grammar Past modals for speculating

Speculating with more certainty

He **must have gone** to his interview.

It was really hot yesterday, so he **couldn't have been** comfortable in a suit.

Speculating with less certainty

He **might have had** a presentation.

He **could have felt** like dressing up.

A Complete the conversations with past modals. Then practice with a partner.

1 A Why hasn't Kate been answering her phone?

B Who knows? She could ________________ (turn) off the ringer.

2 A Why did Randy quit his job yesterday?

B I'm not sure. He might ________________ (get) a better one.

3 A Have you seen Nancy?

B No, she hasn't come to work yet. She could ________________ (oversleep) again.

4 A Is Emma here? She's late for her appointment. That never happens.

B Something important must ________________ (delay) her.

5 A What's wrong? Did Jack forget your birthday?

B He could ________________ (not/forget) it. He always remembers.

B Read the questions in Part A. Write different explanations. Then practice with a partner.

1 ____

2 ____

3 ____

4 ____

5 ____

4 Speaking Possible explanations

GROUP WORK Discuss possible explanations for these situations.

1 Your classmate seemed very forgetful today.

2 Your friend is fluent in Russian after only three months of study.

3 Your friend used to be very careless, but suddenly you can depend on her for anything.

4 Your cousin used to be afraid of animals, but now he is fearless.

"My classmate might have had very little sleep. That could have made him forgetful."

5 Keep talking!

Students A and B go to page 141 and Students C and D go to page 142 for more practice.

I can speculate about everyday situations.

B I'm pretty sure that . . .

1 Interactions Probability and improbability

A PAIR WORK **Try this experiment. Do it ten times, then change roles.**

Student A: Think of a number between 1 and 10.

Student B: Try to read your partner's mind by guessing if the number is *even* (2, 4, 6, . . .) or *odd* (1, 3, 5, . . .).

Did you guess correctly? Who else in the class guessed correctly? How many times?

B **Listen to the conversation. How does Daniela explain mind-reading between twins? Then practice the conversation.**

Daniela I saw a TV show yesterday about twins who read each other's minds. Do you think that's possible?

Jenny Well, twins spend a lot of time together. It's likely that they can read each other's thoughts.

Daniela Really?

Jenny Why not? When they're young, some twins develop a secret language only they understand. That shows that twins can be special.

Daniela But I doubt that anyone can really read minds. They could have guessed each other's thoughts because they spend a lot of time together. But that's not mind reading.

Jenny You are so skeptical.

Daniela I know. So, should we order now?

Jenny You just read my mind!

C **Read the expressions below. Complete each box with a similar expression from the conversation. Then listen and check your answers.**

Expressing probability	Expressing improbability
________________	________________
I'm pretty sure that . . .	It's doubtful that . . .
It's very probable that . . .	It's highly unlikely that . . .

D GROUP WORK **Check (✓) the sentences you think are probable. Then talk to your group about what is probable and what is improbable.**

- ☐ Twins have a special relationship.
- ☐ Twins are more alike than different.
- ☐ Only some people can read minds.
- ☐ All twins can read each other's minds.

2 Listening Likely . . . or unlikely?

A PAIR WORK **Which of these things can help you know what others are thinking?**

body language	emotions	hairstyles	memory
dreams	facial expressions	laughing	tone of voice

B **Listen to Karl tell his friend Jenna about an article on mind-reading. How do people read minds? Look at Part A again, and circle the ways that are mentioned in the article.**

C **Listen to the rest of the conversation. Correct the statements.**

1 Strangers can read each other's minds ~~30%~~ 20% of the time.
2 Married couples can read each other's minds 45% of the time.
3 No one can read minds more than 6% of the time.
4 There's a big difference in how well men and women can read minds.
5 It's likely that Jenna believes what Karl says about men and women.

3 Speaking Anything's possible.

A **Read the statements. Do you think they are probable? Write P (probable) or I (improbable) next to each statement.**

_____ People will travel through time someday.

_____ Some people can remember their past lives.

_____ Some people can predict the weather.

_____ Some people can communicate with animals.

_____ Some people can predict trends in the stock market.

_____ Some people can heal themselves with their mind.

B GROUP WORK **Share your ideas.**

A: *I doubt that people will travel through time someday.*
B: *I agree. It's highly unlikely.*
C: *I'm not so sure. I bet it will happen someday because . . .*

I can express probability and improbability.

C History's mysteries

1 Vocabulary Mysterious events

A Match the words and the stories. Then listen and check your answers.

a	abduction
b	disappearance
c	discovery
d	escape
e	explosion
f	theft

1 ______ In 1962, three men broke out of San Francisco's Alcatraz prison. They were never seen again.

2 ______ In 1908, a huge object from space exploded over Siberia. It destroyed 80 million trees.

3 ______ In 1937, Amelia Earhart disappeared during a flight over the Pacific Ocean. She was never seen again.

4 ______ In 1961, Betty and Barney Hill claimed they were taken aboard a UFO by unfriendly aliens.

5 ______ In 1985, divers found large rocks near Japan that some believe are a lost underwater city.

6 ______ In 1990, robbers in Boston stole paintings worth $300 million. They have never been recovered.

B PAIR WORK Choose three words from Part A. What are other examples of these types of events? Tell your partner.

2 Conversation It remains a mystery.

A Listen to the conversation. What does the tourist learn about the Great Pyramid?

Guide No one really knows how the Egyptian pyramids were built. There are many theories and new discoveries, but it remains a mystery.

Tourist Do you have any idea how long it took to build them?

Guide Yes. It took about 20 years to build the tallest one, the Great Pyramid.

Tourist Can you tell me how tall it is?

Guide It's more than 450 feet, or about 139 meters. It was the tallest structure in the world for thousands of years.

Tourist Really?

Guide Yes. It was the world's tallest structure until the Eiffel Tower was built.

Tourist That's amazing! Do you know how many pyramids were built in Egypt?

Guide No one knows. But at least 80 pyramids have survived, and many more are still under the sand.

B Listen to the rest of the conversation. Why was the Sphinx built? What happened to its nose?

3 Grammar Embedded questions

An embedded question is a question included in another question.	
Wh- questions	**Embedded Wh- questions**
How many pyramids were built?	Do you know **how many pyramids were built?**
How long did it take to build?	Do you have any idea **how long it took to build?**
How tall is the Great Pyramid?	Can you tell me **how tall the Great Pyramid is?**
Yes / no questions	**Embedded yes / no questions**
Was the Sphinx painted?	Do you know **if the Sphinx was painted?**
Are there any chambers?	Can you tell me **if there are any chambers?**
Did its nose fall off?	Do you know **if its nose fell off?**

Rewrite the questions. Use embedded questions. Then compare with a partner.

1 Have there been many thefts from the pyramids?
A Do you know ______________________________? B Yes, many.

2 How long was the Great Pyramid the world's tallest structure?
A Do you know ______________________________? B For 3,800 years.

3 How many chambers are there in the Great Pyramid?
A Can you tell me ______________________________? B There are three.

4 Can tourists climb the Sphinx?
A Do you have any idea ______________________________? B No, it's not allowed.

5 Did aliens build the pyramids?
A Do you know ______________________________? B It's highly unlikely.

4 Pronunciation Intonation in embedded questions

A Listen and repeat. Notice the falling intonation in embedded questions.

Can you tell me how tall it is? Do you know if the Sphinx was painted?

B PAIR WORK Practice the embedded questions in Exercise 3. Pay attention to your intonation.

5 Speaking Endless possibilities

PAIR WORK Discuss possible explanations for the mysteries in Exercise 1.

A: Do you have and idea what happened to Amelia Earhart?

B: No one does. But she might have crashed on an island.

6 Keep talking!

Go to page 143 for more practice.

I can ask and speculate about historical events.

D Unexplained abilities

1 Reading

A **"You don't remember what happened. What you remember becomes what happened." – John Green**
What do you think this quote means? Do you trust your memory?

B **Read the article. Do you think Jill Price views her ability as a gift or a curse?**

THE WOMAN WHO CAN'T FORGET

Jill Price has a powerful memory. She can remember every detail of her life since age 14 — whether she wants to or not. "Since 1980, I remember everything." She remembers where she was, what she felt, what she was wearing, who she was with, what the weather was, and what was in the news.

When she contacted memory researchers in 2000, she was hopeful they could explain her abilities. But they were stumped. After lots of tests, the researchers identified a new medical condition for her called hyperthymesia, meaning "superior memory." Only a handful of people have been diagnosed with the condition.

Does she remember when the big plane crash in Scotland occurred? "December 21, 1988." Can she recall the first time she heard the song, "Jessie's Girl"? "March 7, 1981." She was driving in a car with her mother. Does she know what she was doing on August 29, 1980? "It was a Friday," she says. She went on a trip to the desert with her friends. Scientists have checked her memories against news reports and her own diaries. Her memories are right almost every time.

"I walk around with my life right next to me," said Price, who lives in California. "I always explain it to people like I'm walking around with a video camera on my shoulder. And every day is a videotape. So if you throw a date out at me, it's as if I pulled a videotape out...and just watch the day."

She doesn't remember everything — only things that happened in her own life. School was awful for her, she says, because she had problems remembering facts and numbers. "I can't look at a phone book and memorize names. I don't do that."

Sometimes she might like to forget, especially when bad things happen in her life. "I still feel bad about stuff that happened 30 years ago," Price said. "It's not as though I'm looking back on the events with the distance of time and adult perspective; it's as though I'm actually living through them again."

Price's condition reminds us that it's probable our happiness might not only depend on what we remember, but what we are able to forget.

C **Read the story again. Answer the questions.**

1 Since what year does Jill Price remember every day of her life? ______
2 What kinds of things does Jill remember? ______
3 What thing does Jill have trouble remembering? ______
4 How many people have been diagnosed with the same condition as Jill? ______
5 How does Jill describe the experience of remembering a day in her life? ______
6 How do scientists know her memory is correct? ______

D PAIR WORK **Would you want to be able to remember everything? Why or why not?**

2 Listening "The Magpies and the Bell"

A Listen to a story from South Korea. Number the pictures from 1 to 6.

B Listen again. Answer the questions.

1 Where was the man going? __________

2 Who was the woman that the man met at the house? __________

3 What did the snake tell the man to do? __________

4 Who saved the man? How? Why? __________

C What lesson about life do you think the story tells?

3 Writing and speaking A story

A Think of a story in your culture that explains something. What does it explain? How does the story explain it?

B Write the story, or retell the story in Exercise 2. Use the model paragraph to help you.

C GROUP WORK Share your stories. Are there any similarities among your stories? Are there any similarities to other stories you know?

The Sleep Tree, a Myth

One day, a man in the rain forest saw a huge, old tree he'd never seen before. Its roots went deep into the ground, and its branches spread all across the sky. The man was amazed. He saw a large group of animals sleeping under the old tree. . .

I can discuss the power of memory.

Wrap-up

1 Quick pair review

Lesson A Do you remember?

How certain are the sentences? Write M (more certain) or L (less certain). You have one minute.

_____ 1 Tom might have been sick yesterday.

_____ 2 The glass must have fallen off the table and broken.

_____ 3 Wendy couldn't have had lunch with Michael yesterday.

_____ 4 Lola could have been at the party.

_____ 5 The storm might have started in Florida.

Lesson B Give your opinion!

What do you think? Use phrases of probability and improbability. Discuss your answers and give your reasons. You have two minutes.

1 Will cars run on water one day?

2 Will people be able to control the weather?

3 Will we find life on other planets?

A: *Do you think cars will run on water one day?*

B: *It's highly unlikely. There isn't enough energy in water. What do you think?*

Lesson C Test your partner!

Say four questions. Can your partner write them as embedded questions? Take turns. You have three minutes.

"Where is Sheila?"

1 *Do you know where Sheila is?* 3 _______________

2 _______________ 4 _______________

Lesson D Brainstorm!

Make up myths about one of the items with a partner. Be creative! You have three minutes.

why fish live in the ocean	why snakes don't have legs	why the sky is blue

A: *A long time ago the sky was white, but a boy found blueberries, and threw them in the sky. It turned the sky blue.*

B: *The sky was black, but when it rained for the first time, it turned blue.*

2 In the real world

Why are these animals unusual? Go online and find information in English about one of them. Then write about them. What do they look like? Where do they live? What do they eat?

- tree kangaroos
- albino snakes
- magpies
- wombats

Tree Kangaroos

Tree kangaroos are unusual because they live in trees. They have shorter legs than most kangaroos. They live in Australia and Papua New Guinea.

10 Perspectives

LESSON A

- Three-word phrasal verbs
- Reported statements

LESSON B

- Changing the topic
- Returning to a topic

LESSON C

- Verbs + prepositions
- Reported *yes* / *no* questions

LESSON D

- Reading: "The Dress" - A Lecture for Professor Lin's Psychology Class
- Writing: Questionnaire results

Warm Up

A Look at the pictures. What do you see? What is the most unusual perspective?

B Do you always see things the same way as your friends?

A A traffic accident

1 Vocabulary Three-word phrasal verbs

A Match the statements in columns A and B. Then listen and check your answers.

A

1 I like to **catch up with** friends online. ____
2 I can **come up with** imaginative ideas. ____
3 I **look up to** my father. ____
4 I **get along with** everybody. ____
5 It's hard to **keep up with** my friends. ____
6 I think that too many people **get away with** speeding. ____
7 I cannot **put up with** people who lie. ____
8 I try to **take care of** my car. ____
9 I always look forward to Sunday mornings. ____

B

a. I really respect him.
b. We chat several times a week.
c. I'm a very creative person.
d. The police should give more tickets.
e. People think I'm very friendly.
f. We don't have time to get together.
g. I change the oil every six months.
h. I love to sleep late on weekends.
i. I get very angry when people don't tell the truth.

B PAIR WORK **Which statements in Part A are true for you? Discuss your answers.**

"It's hard to keep up with my friends. I have a lot of friends because I get along with everybody."

2 Language in context Whose fault was it?

A Read the traffic accident report that the police officer wrote. What did the witness see?

Traffic Accident Report

Mrs. Fran Perry, 35, hit a traffic light pole on the corner of First and Lexington at 6:45 this evening. She said she had turned quickly to avoid a dog. The pole was not damaged, but her car had a broken light. She said she would take care of it right away.

Mr. Jerry Thomas, 62, told an officer he'd seen the accident from his bedroom window. He saw a man who had taken his dog off its leash. He said the driver had been on her cell phone.

Both the driver and the witness said that they would come in and make a full statement.

B What about you? Who do you feel is more responsible for the accident – the driver or the dog owner? Why?

3 Grammar Reported statements

Use reported speech to tell what a speaker has said without using the person's exact words. When using reported speech, you often have to change pronouns and the tense of the verb.

Direct speech	Reported speech
"I **am** in a hurry."	She **told me** (that) she **was** in a hurry.
"I **am telling** the truth."	She **told me** (that) she **was telling** the truth.
"I **have** an appointment."	She **told me** (that) she **had** an appointment.
"I **saw** the accident."	He **said** (that) he **had seen** the accident.
"The dog **has disappeared**."	He **said** (that) the dog **had disappeared**.
"We **will make** a statement."	They **said** (that) they **would make** a statement.

A Complete the report with *said* or *told*. Then compare with a partner.

Car Accident on Main St.

Last night, Darren Jones, 18, was riding his bicycle when a car suddenly stopped in front of him. He crashed his bicycle into the car. Darren ____________ police that he hadn't seen it stop. He ____________ police he was sorry, but he ____________ it hadn't been his fault. The driver, Lacey Reed, 45, ____________ that she had stopped because a man was crossing the road. A witness, James Lee, 68, ____________ police he had seen everything. Everyone ____________ they would make a formal report.

B Rewrite these sentences. Use reported speech. Then compare with a partner.

1 Lacey said, "I want to call my husband." *Lacey said she wanted to call her husband.*
2 Darren told me, "It's not my fault." *Darren told me* ____________
3 James told me, "I heard a loud crash." ____________
4 James said, "I have seen accidents here before." ____________
5 Lacey told me, "I'll take care of the bills." ____________

4 Speaking What did he say?

A Choose one question. Write the answer in one sentence.

- What do you do to catch up with your friends?
- What are you looking forward to doing?
- How do you keep up with the news?

B GROUP WORK Whisper your sentence to the person on your right. That person whispers your sentence to the person on the right. Continue until the sentence is reported back to you. Was it your sentence, or was it different?

A: *I'm looking forward to graduating next year.*

B: *Jason told me he was looking forward to graduating next year.*

C: *Maria said that Jason was looking forward to . . .*

5 Keep talking!

Student A go to page 144 and
Student B go to page 146 for more practice.

I can report what people say.

B As I was saying . . .

1 Interactions Changing and returning to the topic

A **Do you enjoy sports? Which do you prefer, watching sports live or on TV? Why? Have you ever disagreed with a referee's call?**

B **Listen to the conversation. What topics are they discussing? Then practice the conversation.**

Maria I don't believe it!

Kate What?

Maria He used his hands. That goal shouldn't have counted.

Kate Are you sure he used his hands?

Maria He did. I saw it clearly.

Kate That reminds me, did you see the game last weekend? I didn't see it, but my brother told me that the same player had scored the winning goal. They won 1-0.

Maria No, I missed it. But as I was saying, I don't think that was a real goal.

Kate Maybe the referee just didn't see it. I know it happens sometimes.

Maria That's possible. Referees are only human, after all.

C **Read the expressions below. Complete each box with a similar expression from the conversation. Then listen and check your answers.**

Changing the topic	Returning to a topic
______________	______________
By the way . . .	To finish what I was saying . . .
I just thought of something.	To get back to what I was saying . . .

D **Number the sentences from 1 to 6. Then practice with a partner.**

_____ A I know. It was. I wish I could go to the game next Sunday, but I don't have tickets. And I have to –

_____ A I can't. Because to finish what I was saying, I have to study all weekend.

_____ A Did you see the soccer game last night?

_____ B I did. I watched it on TV. It was awesome.

_____ B That's too bad. But I have tickets for the game the following weekend, too. Want to go then?

_____ B Hang on. I just thought of something. I have two tickets! Want to go?

2 Pronunciation Linked vowel sounds with /w/ and /y/

A Listen and repeat. Notice how the vowel sounds at the beginning and end of words are linked with a /w/ sound or a /y/ sound.

/w/	/w/	/w/	/y/	/y/	/y/
know if	do it	go over	say anything	see it	I am

B Listen. Write 'w' or 'y' over the linked sounds. Then practice with a partner.

/ /	/ /	/ /	/ /	/ /	/ /
pay any	how exactly	be in	too old	no one	who is

3 Listening Sports talk

A Listen to three conversations between Alex and Celia. What do they discuss in each conversation? Check (✓) the answers.

	What do they begin to discuss?	What is the topic changed to?
1	☐ extreme sports ☐ the dangers of sports	
2	☐ sports on TV ☐ the Olympics	
3	☐ sports fads ☐ sports fans	

B Listen again. What is the topic changed to in each conversation? Write the topics in the chart.

4 Speaking Stick to the topic

A Choose one of these topics or another related to sports. Prepare to talk about it for at least a minute.

extreme sports	a great team
ads in sports	sports equipment
benefits of sports	sports fads
a great athlete	sports fans

B GROUP WORK Take turns. Discuss your topic. The other students keep trying to change the topic. Return to your topic each time.

A: *I think snowboarding is an amazing extreme sport.*

B: *I agree. You know, that reminds me, did you see the ice skating at the Olympics this year?*

A: *Um, no. I couldn't watch the games. But as I was saying, snowboarding is really . . .*

I can change and return to the topic.

C There's always an explanation.

1 Vocabulary Verbs + prepositions

A Match the verbs and the prepositions. Add the verbs to the chart. Then listen and check your answers.

believe	depend	forget	participate	rely
decide	dream	hear	plan	worry

about		on		in

B PAIR WORK Complete these questions with the correct prepositions. Ask and answer the questions. Do you see things the same way?

1 Do you believe ______________ UFOs?
2 Who do you rely ______________ the most?
3 What do you plan ______________ doing in the future?
4 What's the most important news event you have heard ______________ recently?
5 What did you dream ______________ last night?
6 Do you participate ______________ any community organizations?

2 Conversation Strange behavior

A Listen to the conversation. Who do you think Chad is?

Gina I'm worried. Chad's been acting strangely.
Marissa What do you mean?
Gina Well, I asked him if he wanted to see a movie on Friday. He told me he couldn't, but he wouldn't say why.
Marissa That's odd.
Gina Then last night he asked me if I was free for dinner on Saturday and if I'd ever been to Michel's.
Marissa I've heard about Michel's. It's one of the nicest places in town.
Gina I know. We never go to places like that. We usually just get a pizza and sodas as takeout.
Marissa Well, I wouldn't worry about it. Just enjoy your dinner.

B Listen to a phone conversation between Marissa and Chad. What did Chad do on Friday night? What's he planning to do on Saturday night?

3 Grammar Reported *yes / no* questions

Use reported yes / no *questions to tell what a speaker has asked without using the person's exact words. When using reported* yes / no *questions you often have to change pronouns and the tense of the verb.*

Direct questions	Reported questions
"**Are** you free for dinner?"	He asked me if I **was** free for dinner.
"**Are** you **having** a good day?"	He asked me if I **was having** a good day.
"**Do** you **want** to see a movie?"	He asked me if I **wanted** to see a movie.
"**Did** you **speak** to your mother?"	He asked me if I **had spoken** to my mother.
"**Have** you **been** to Michel's?"	He asked me if I **had been** to Michel's.
"**Will** you **marry** me?"	He asked me if I **would marry** him.

Rewrite the questions. Use reported questions. Then compare with a partner.

1 Marissa asked Chad, "Have you spoken to Gina yet?"
Marissa asked Chad if he had spoken to Gina yet.

2 Marissa asked Chad, "Are you planning on asking Gina to marry you?"
____

3 Marissa asked Chad, "Are you worried about Gina's answer?"
____

4 Chad asked Marissa, "Will Gina say yes?"
____

5 Gina asked Marissa, "Do you believe in love at first sight?"
____

6 Marissa asked Gina, "Did you dream about the perfect wedding as a child?"
____

7 Marissa asked Gina, "Have you already decided on a wedding date?"
____

4 Speaking Ask me anything!

A CLASS ACTIVITY **Imagine you are someone famous. Walk around the class. Find out who your classmates are. Ask and answer *yes / no* questions.**

A: *Hello. I'm Will Smith.*

B: *Can I ask you a question? Do you participate in any charities?*

B GROUP WORK **Report the most interesting questions and answers.**

"Francesca asked me if I participated in any charities. I told her I had participated in a lot of charities – especially ones that work with safe water."

5 Keep talking!

Go to page 145 for more practice.

I can report what people ask.

D Seeing things differently

1 Reading

A What color is the dress below? How certain are you?

B Read the lecture by Professor Lin. What is the real color of the dress?

"THE DRESS" – A Lecture for Professor Lin's Psychology Class

Do you remember this meme from a few years ago? A young woman posted a picture of this dress online. She said she and her friends couldn't decide on what color it was. The image went viral. Within 10 hours, an online poll had received 1.8 million votes. About 72% of people reported that they saw white and gold and 28% saw black and blue. The question on everyone's mind was, how is that possible?

The dress is actually black and blue, but nearly three out of four people saw the wrong colors. *Here's why:*

Figure 1

Figure 2

Scientists think that our perception of color depends on our perception of lighting. For example, look at Figure 2 – the squares marked A and B are exactly the same color, but because the B square looks like it's in shadow and is where a lighter square should be, our brain tells us it's a lighter shade.

Now, looking at the picture of the dress, we don't know how it is lit. Is it natural light or artificial light? Is it in shadow? Our brains are really good at filling in details we don't know, so we make assumptions about the color of the lighting. People who assume the dress is in shadow or lit by natural light (which has more blue in it) tend to subtract the blue tones in the photo and see the dress as white and gold. People who assume the lighting is artificial (which has more yellow) assume the dress is black and blue.

The next question is, why do some people assume the dress is lit by natural light and others assume artificial light? Scientists think it may have to do with when we get up and go to sleep. People who are early risers spend more time in natural daylight and might assume the dress is lit by that same light. People who are night owls and are awake more at night might assume the dress is lit by the artificial light they spend more time in.

So the lesson is, whenever you're absolutely sure the way you see things is right, remember that there's a possibility that others have a perfectly good explanation for why they see it differently!

C Read the dialogue again. Answer the questions using reported speech.

1. Why did the original user post the photo? *She said she and her friends couldn't decide on the color.*
2. How many votes did the poll receive? ______
3. How did scientists explain the difference in people's perception of color? ______
4. What did Professor Lin say our brains are really good at? ______
5. According to scientists, who might assume the dress is lit by artificial light? ______

D PAIR WORK What are other things that people see very differently? Can you imagine why they might have different opinions?

2 Listening Justin's turn

A Listen to Allie ask her friend Justin some of the questions from a questionnaire. Number them from 1 to 5 in the order she asks them.

Questions	Answers
☐ What is your greatest fear?	
☐ What is your idea of perfect happiness?	
☐ What word do you most overuse?	
☐ What is your current state of mind?	
☐ What is your greatest regret?	

B Listen again. Write Justin's answers.

3 Writing Questionnaire results

A Choose any two questions from Exercise 2, and write them in the chart. Think about your answers. Then ask each question to two classmates and write their answers.

	Questions	Name: ________	Name: ________
1			
2			

B Write about the questionnaire results in Part A. Use the model to help you.

> **Questionnaire Results**
>
> The three of us have very different regrets. Eun-ju said her greatest regret was quitting piano lessons. Antonio said that his was not listening to his grandfather's advice. I think my greatest regret is something I said to my brother once . . .

C GROUP WORK Share your writing with your classmates.

4 Speaking Imagine that!

A Look at the questions below. Think about your own answers.

- If you could have one superpower, what would it be?
- What famous person do you think you look like?
- What song title best describes your feelings about life?
- If you could be any animal for a day, what would you be?
- If a movie were made about your life, what would the title be?

B PAIR WORK Ask your partner the questions in Part A. Write the answers.

C GROUP WORK Report the most interesting information you found out.

I can discuss different perspectives. ✓

Wrap-up

1 Quick pair review

Lesson A Test your partner!

Say four sentences to your partner using direct speech. Can your partner say the sentences using reported speech? Take turns. You and your partner have one minute.

A: *My sister will take good care of my dog.*

B: *You told me that your sister would take good care of your dog.*

Lesson B Do you remember?

Complete the expressions for changing a topic and returning to a topic. Circle the correct words. You have one minute.

1 I **back / just** thought of something.
2 By the **way / what**, I saw a concert on Friday.
3 That **says / reminds** me, are you driving to work tomorrow?
4 As I was **saying / finishing** I look up to my teachers. They work very hard.
5 To finish **way / what** I was saying, let's have Chinese food.
6 To get **me / back** to what I was saying, Carly gets along with everybody.

Lesson C Find out!

Who is one person both you and your partner depend on? Worry about a lot? Have heard about recently in the news? Plan on visiting soon? You and your partner have two minutes.

A: *I depend on my brother. He's older and knows a lot of things. What about you?*

B: *I don't have a brother. But I depend on my father. Do you?*

A: *Yes, I do.*

Lesson D Give your opinion!

Who are people that you could describe using these phrases? You have two minutes.

a talented athlete ______	an amazing singer ______
a hardworking actor ______	a quick thinker ______
a friendly teacher ______	a confident woman ______

2 In the real world

Whose side are you on? Go online and find information in English about one of these topics. Then write about it. What do people think about it? What do you think?

- art made from recycled trash
- extreme sports
- hybrid cars
- reality shows

Trash Art

Many people think art made from recycled trash is good for the environment. Other people think it's ugly.

I agree with both opinions. It is good for the environment, but it's usually ugly!

11 The real world

LESSON A
- Word partners
- Causative *get* and *have*

LESSON B
- Taking time to think
- Closing an interview

LESSON C
- Setting goals
- Future continuous vs. future with *will*

LESSON D
- Reading: "Jobs of the Future"
- Writing: A letter of interest

Warm Up

A Match the jobs and the pictures.

1 animal trainer
2 archaeologist
3 DJ
4 fashion designer
5 hairstylist
6 race-car driver
7 singer / songwriter
8 tour guide
9 social media marketer

B What three jobs do you think would be the most interesting? What would you like about them? Why?

A Getting it done

1 Vocabulary Word partners

A **Cross out the words that do not go together. Then listen and check your answers.**

1	accept	a job offer / ~~a job ad~~
2	apply for	a letter / a job
3	format	an interview / a résumé
4	prepare for	a business card / an interview
5	print	an email / a job
6	proofread	a résumé / a job offer
7	provide	a company / references
8	research	a job / a résumé
9	send	a thank-you note / a phone call
10	translate	a job / a letter

B PAIR WORK **Ask and answer the questions.**

1. If you were looking for a job, what things in Part A would you do?
2. Have you ever applied for a job? What was it?
3. What would you include on your résumé?

2 Language in context Tips from a recruiter

A **Read the tips from a recruiter to job hunters. Which tip should you do after the interview?**

Find references
Get people that you trust to provide references for you.

Invest in your résumé
Get your résumé formatted, proofread, and printed on good quality paper.

Prepare for the interview
Have a friend prepare possible interview questions. Practice answering them

Know the way
Research directions to the interview site and have someone drive you there.

Don't be late
Arrive at the interview site at least 15 minutes before the interview.

Look your best
Have your best clothes dry-cleaned and pressed. Dress for success!

Remember to smile
Show a pleasant face the minute you walk into the interview. Keep smiling.

Do the research
Research the job and the company. Ask questions about information that is not found on the company's website.

Say thanks
Send a short thank-you note or email to the person or people who interviewed you.

B **What about you? Are all the tips appropriate in your culture? What other tips can you add?**

3 Grammar Causative *get* and *have*

get + someone + to + *verb* **Get** people to **provide** references for you. get + someone + *verb* I plan to **have** a friend **practice** with me.	get + something + *past participle* Where can I **get** my résumé **printed**? Have + something + *past participle* I need to **have** my clothes **dry-cleaned**.

A Circle the correct words. Then compare with a partner.

1 My company is trying to get Greg **accept** / **to accept** / **accepted** our job offer.
2 I need to have someone **translate** / **to translate** / **translated** my résumé into English.
3 I'd like to get my former boss **provide** / **to provide** / **provided** a reference letter.
4 You should have your suit **dry-clean** / **to dry-clean** / **dry-cleaned** before the interview.
5 Where can I get some business cards **print** / **to print** / **printed**?

B Put the words in order. Then compare with a partner.

1 Paul / his brother / gets / his hair / cut / to — Paul gets his brother to cut his hair.
2 I / to / a reference letter / got / write / my boss — I ______.
3 Where / have / proofread / I / can / my résumé — Where ______?
4 Jay / his house / on Saturday / had / cleaned — Jay ______.
5 Liz / to get / proofread / her presentation / needs — Liz ______.

4 Listening So much to do!

A Listen to three busy people talk about their plans. Write what they are going to do themselves.

	Do themselves	Have or get done
1		
2		
3		

B Listen again. Write one thing each person is going to have or get done.

5 Speaking Do it yourself?

GROUP WORK Imagine you are preparing for an interview. Look at the "to do" list. What would you do yourself? What would you have or get done? Share your ideas.

○	cut my hair	iron my shirt	proofread my résumé
○	dry-clean my suit	photocopy my résumé	take photos
○	format my résumé	print business cards	translate my résumé

A: I'd format my résumé, but I'd get someone else to proofread it.

B: Me, too. I'd have my résumé translated, and then I'd photocopy it myself.

6 Keep talking!

Go to page 147 for more practice.

I can talk about getting things done.

B Let me see . . .

1 Interactions Interviewing

A Imagine you've applied for a job at a company and are preparing for an interview. What topics do you think you would discuss in the interview?

benefits	hours	salary	your education
break times	retirement plan	travel opportunities	your skills and abilities

B Listen to the conversation. How does Mr. Reed describe himself? Practice the conversation.

Interviewer	I just have a few more questions, Mr. Reed. Why do you want to work here?
Mr. Reed	I'd like to get some experience in this field and put my skills to work.
Interviewer	And what are your best skills?
Mr. Reed	Oh, let's see. . .I'm responsible, hardworking, and can work independently.
Interviewer	That's good. Can you work weekends?
Mr. Reed	Sure. That's not a problem.
Interviewer	Can you provide references?
Mr. Reed	Of course.
Interviewer	Well, it's been nice meeting you. I want to thank you for coming in for this interview.
Mr. Reed	Thank you very much.

C Read the expressions below. Complete each box with a similar expression from the conversation. Then listen and check your answers.

Taking time to think

____

Um, let me see . . .

Hmm, let me think . . .

Closing an interview

____

Well, it's been great talking to you.

Well, I've really enjoyed talking to you.

D Number the sentences from 1 to 8. Then practice with a partner.

_____ A You're welcome. We'll be in touch.

__1__ A So, what skills do you have?

_____ A Good. Well, it's been nice meeting you.

_____ A That's good. What's the earliest you can start?

_____ B Thank you for the interview.

_____ B Good-bye. Thank you again.

_____ B Um, let me see. I could start in a week.

_____ B I'm good with people, and I can use all of the latest office software.

2 Listening Getting the job?

A **Listen to the last part of a job interview. Check (✓) the job the man is most likely applying for.**

☐ TV host ☐ soccer coach ☐ radio DJ ☐ translator ☐ scientist

B **Listen again. How does the man answer the interviewer's questions? Complete the interviewer's notes.**

1	What skills do you have?	______ and asking questions
2	What would you like about the job?	the ______ ______
3	What is your greatest strength?	______ skills
4	What is your greatest weakness?	doesn't ______ some current ______
5	What is your career goal?	host TV ______ ______
6	Can you work weekends?	can work ______ but not ______

C PAIR WORK **Did the man interview well? Why or why not?**

3 Speaking Help wanted

A **Prepare for a job interview. Choose one of the jobs. Think of answers to the questions below.**

JOBS

MAGAZINE COLUMNIST

Trendy magazine seeks outgoing person to write weekly column on what's hot around town. Latest knowledge of music, food, movies, and fashion required. Must be able to write quickly under pressure. Pay per word.

ASSISTANT COACH

Energetic and patient person needed to work as part-time assistant to head coach at local high school. No experience necessary. Strong ability in several sports desired. Applicant must be a team player. Pay negotiable.

ONLINE TUTOR

Work from home! Reliable tutor needed to teach English and / or math to high school students online. Must have own phone and computer and be able to work independently. Flexible hours. Hourly pay. Perfect for college students.

- Can you tell me a little about yourself?
- What skills do you have?
- What is your greatest strength?
- What is your greatest weakness?
- What is your career goal?
- Can you work weekends?
- How would your friends describe you?
- How do you cope with stress?

B PAIR WORK **Role-play the job interview for a job in Part A. Then change roles.**

Student A: Tell your partner which job you have chosen. Answer Student B's questions. Take time to think when you need to.

Student B: Interview Student A. Ask the questions in Part A and questions of your own. Then close the interview.

I can take time to think in an interview. ✓

I can close an interview. ✓

C Future goals

1 Vocabulary Setting goals

A 🎧 **Match the words and the pictures. Then listen and check your answers.**

a	be financially independent	c	have a big wedding	e	prepare for my exams	g	work as a journalist
b	do volunteer work	d	live in the countryside	f	study abroad	h	write travel books

1 ☐

2 ☐

3 ☐

4 ☐

5 ☐

6 ☐

7 ☐

8 ☐

B PAIR WORK **Do you have any of these goals? Which ones? Have you already reached any of these goals? Tell your partner.**

2 Conversation Planning ahead

A 🎧 **Listen to the conversation. Who will Zac marry in five years?**

Zac Guess what! I've decided to study abroad next year. At this time next year, I'll be studying in Paris!

Lucy Really? That sounds wonderful.

Zac I've been thinking a lot lately about what I want to achieve in my life. In five years, I'll be working as a journalist. In seven years, I'll be living in the countryside. In twenty years –

Lucy But what about family? Will you get married?

Zac Oh, yes. I'll have a big wedding in five years.

Lucy OK . . . and who will you marry?

Zac I have no idea. But I'm sure I'll meet someone.

B 🎧 **Listen to the rest of the conversation. What two things is Lucy doing these days? What job does she think she'll have in five years?**

3 Grammar Future continuous vs. future with *will*

Use the future continuous form to describe actions in progress at a specific time in the future.
Where **will** you **be studying** next year?
I**'ll be studying** in Paris. I **won't be working** as a journalist then.
Use the future with will *verbs that are not usually used in the continuous form.*
What **will** you **achieve** in twenty years? **Will** you **be** financially independent?
Yes, I **will**. But I**'ll have to** work really hard.

Complete the conversations with the future continuous or future with *will*. Then practice with a partner.

1 A What ____________ you ____________ (do) a year from now?
B I ____________ (study) abroad.
2 A What ____________ (happen) to your friends after graduation?
B Sam and Ann ____________ (have) a big wedding. Jacob ____________ (work) in the city.
3 A Where ____________ you ____________ (live) in ten years?
B I don't know, but I probably ____________ (not / live) here.
4 A What ____________ your life ____________ (be) like in the future?
B I ____________ (not / work) for a large company. I ____________ (write) travel books.
5 A ____________ you ____________ (go) on vacation in July?
B Yes, I ____________ (go) to Rome. I ____________ (see) the Colosseum and the Trevi Fountain.

4 Pronunciation Reduction of *will*

A Listen and repeat. Notice how *will* often gets reduced to 'll after *Wh-* question words and nouns.

When will your friends finish this class? What will they be doing afterwards?
John will still be studying, and Beth will be looking for a job.

B PAIR WORK Practice the questions and answers in Exercise 3A. Pay attention to the reduction of *will*.

5 Speaking My own goals

A What goals do you have? When do you hope to reach those goals?

B GROUP WORK Share your goals. Ask and answer questions to get more information.

A: I'll be married in five years. I think I'll be working for a large company.
B: What kind of large company will you be working for?

6 Keep talking!

Go to page 148 for more practice.

I can ask and talk about future goals.

D My career

1 Reading

A **The jobs of today may not be the jobs of the future. Which of these jobs do you think will exist in the future? Will they be different in any way? Which will disappear? Why?**

cashier	doctor	farmer	pilot	reporter	soldier	teacher	travel agent

B **Read the article. What is it about? Check (✓) the main idea.**

☐ jobs that will appear ☐ jobs that will disappear ☐ current jobs that will stay the same

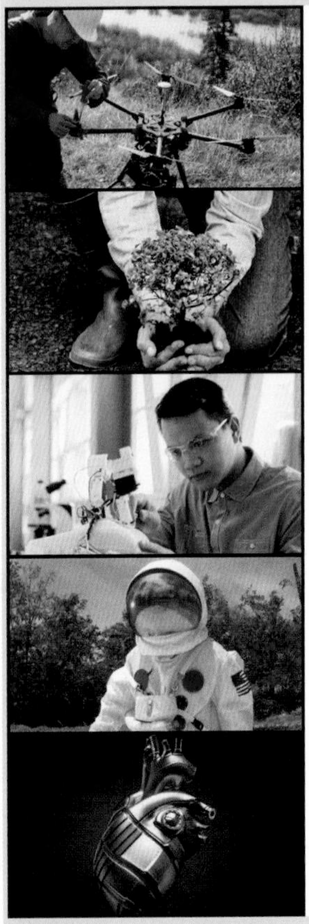

JOBS OF THE FUTURE

Drone Manager – More businesses and government agencies will be relying on drones to take video from the air, or even to deliver packages. Companies will need drone managers to keep track of all their drones, to make sure they operate within the law and don't cause damage or injuries.

Rewilder – Rewilders will help to repair environmental damage by returning developed areas to their natural state. From tearing down buildings and ripping up roads to replacing industrial areas with forests, rewilders will be undoing the damage that buildings, cars, factories, and human beings have done to the planet.

Robot Technician – Nearly half of all jobs today will be taken over by robots during this century. Companies will have robots to repair watches, make phone calls, sew clothing, and handle many other routine tasks. Robot programmers and technicians will be needed to tell the robots what to do and to take care of the mechanical problems that these robots will certainly have.

Space Tour Guide – More and more people will be taking vacations in space, and they will need tour guides. Several companies have already begun space programs with trips that cost between $75,000 and $2 million. In the future, these high prices should become more affordable, and more space guides will be needed.

Organ Designers – Millions of people today are waiting for new hearts, lungs, livers, and other organs. In the future, organ manufacturers will be making artificial organs, organs grown in a laboratory from a patient's own cells, or combinations of both. Organs will be designed to fit each individual patient.

C **Check (✓) the true sentences. Then correct the false ones.**

☐ 1 A drone manager may be a needed job in the future. ____________

☐ 2 Rewilders will help build new roads and factories. ____________

☐ 3 Robots will take over almost all future jobs. ____________

☐ 4 Space travel for tourists has already begun. ____________

☐ 5 Organs will be made only from a patient's own cells. ____________

D PAIR WORK **Which of the jobs in the article do you think is most likely to be a popular career? What qualifications would someone need for these jobs? Discuss your ideas.**

2 Writing and speaking A letter of interest

A Read these job ads for positions at Carolina Industries. Then read the letter below. What job is Teresa interested in?

Tech Support Officer
Maintain and ensure smooth running of computer systems and internal network. Must be familiar with latest hardware and software. Flexible hours.

Recruiter
Find, interview, and test applicants to locate qualified employees for job openings. Must be organized and able to travel to colleges and job fairs.

Marketing Assistant
Entry-level job for recent graduate. Assist staff in Marketing Department. Duties include filing, research, and working with new customers.

Your address	Portal Bravo #19D 37529 Leon, Mexico
Date	June 7, 2019
Name, title, company, and address of the person you're writing to	Ms. Susan Dodd Personnel Manager Carolina Industries 662 Beacon Road Salt Lake City, Utah 84110
Try to use the name of the person.	Dear Ms. Dodd:
State why you are writing.	I would like to express my interest in the marketing assistant job recently advertised on your website.
Briefly state your education and any experience or skills.	I will be graduating next month with a B.A. in Marketing from Monterrey University. I am fluent in English and Spanish, with a basic knowledge of Japanese. Enclosed is my résumé, which contains detailed information on my education and experience.
Say how you can be contacted.	I would appreciate the opportunity to discuss this position with you. I can be reached by cell phone at 319-555-8116 or by email at teresasanchez@cup.org.
Thank the person.	Thank you very much for your time and consideration.
Use a formal closing.	Sincerely,
Sign your name.	*Theresa Sanchez* Theresa Sanchez

B Choose a job from this lesson or use your own idea. Write a letter of interest.

C GROUP WORK Share your letters. What kinds of jobs are your classmates interested in? What do you think they will be doing in five years?

A: *Jean is interested in the tech support job.*

B: *Really? I think Jean will be working as a space tour guide in the future, not a tech support officer. She's so friendly and outgoing.*

I can discuss future careers. ✓

Wrap-up

1 Quick pair review

Lesson A Find out!

What are two things both you and your partner usually have done or get done? You and your partner have two minutes.

A: I get my photos printed at the drugstore.

B: Really? I print my pictures on my computer. I usually have my nice clothes dry-cleaned. What about you?

A: Yes. I do, too.

Lesson B Do you remember?

What can you say when you need time to think? Check (✓) the correct answers. You have one minute.

_____ 1 Oh, let's see.

_____ 2 Well, it's been great talking to you.

_____ 3 I'm not sure that's really true.

_____ 4 Oh, really?

_____ 5 Um, let me see.

_____ 6 Hmm, let me think.

Lesson C Guess!

Describe something you will be doing in the future, but don't say where it will be. Can your partner guess the place? You have two minutes.

A: I'll be sitting in the sun in two months, and I'll be swimming in the ocean.

B: Will you be on vacation? Will you be going to the beach?

A: Yes, I will.

Lesson D Give your opinion!

How important will these jobs be in 50 years? Rank them from 1 (the most important) to 8 (the least important). Compare your answers. You have three minutes.

_____ computer programmer	_____ lawyer
_____ librarian	_____ TV host
_____ English teacher	_____ flight attendant
_____ art teacher	_____ chef

2 In the real world

How can you prepare for jobs of the future? Go to a university website. See what classes they offer, such as video-game design, robotics, or solar energy. Then write about a job of the future.

Preparing for Jobs of the Future

In the future, most jobs will be high-tech. Everyone will have to study math and science to get a good job. I want to design video games, so I will . . .

12 Finding solutions

LESSON A
- Preventing pollution
- Present continuous passive; infinitive passive

LESSON B
- Supporting an opinion
- Not supporting an opinion

LESSON C
- Community improvement
- Linking words

LESSON D
- Reading: "El Sistema: Social Change Through Music"
- Writing: A letter to a community leader

"It's just their little way of saying, 'Sorry we wrecked the planet.'"

Warm Up

A Describe the cartoons. What are the problems in each cartoon?

B How do you feel about the problems?

A Environmental concerns

1 Vocabulary Preventing pollution

A Match the **bold** words and their meanings. Then listen and check your answers.

Ways of preventing air pollution

1 **Combine** tasks if you drive. ______
2 **Commute** by bicycle if possible. ______
3 **Maintain** your car so that it's more efficient. ______
4 **Avoid** products that come in spray cans. ______

a. don't use
b. go to work
c. do together
d. keep in good condition

Ways of preventing water pollution

5 **Store** paint and chemicals in safe containers. ______
6 **Limit** your use of harmful cleaning products. ______
7 **Discard** paint and batteries properly. ______
8 **Conserve** water whenever possible. ______

e. save
f. put or keep
g. throw away
h. control the amount

Ways of preventing land pollution

9 **Purchase** products with little packaging. ______
10 **Recycle** any item you can. ______
11 **Identify** where trash cans are. ______
12 Never **dump** motor oil on the ground. ______

i. use again
j. find or locate
k. put carelessly
l. buy

B PAIR WORK Which things in Part A do you think you could do? Which do you already do? Tell your partner.

2 Language in context Promoting "green" travel

A Read about a high-tech solution to traveling "green." What problem did it solve?

Bicycles are being parked in a whole new way in Tokyo. Commuters used to leave their bicycles on the sidewalks outside train stations, but people couldn't move around them and something clearly had to be done. Now, at Kasai Station, commuters can leave their bikes in a 10-level underground parking garage that is controlled by robots. Robots store nearly 10,000 bicycles a day. When commuters want their bicycles, they use cards to identify them. Within seconds, a robot finds and brings it to them. The Tokyo garage is so successful that more "green" garages are being considered.

B How does the underground parking garage help "green" travel? Could Tokyo's solution work for you?

3 Grammar Present continuous passive; infinitive passive

Use the present continuous passive to describe an action in progress when you want to focus on the receiver of the action instead of on the doer of the action.

Active	*Passive*
Commuters **are parking** bicycles in a new way.	Bicycles **are being parked** in a new way.

Use the infinitive passive after verbs like have and need when you want to focus on the receiver of the action instead of the doer of the action.

Active	*Passive*
Somebody **had to do** something.	Something **had to be done**.
People **needed to put** the bikes somewhere.	The bikes **needed to be put** somewhere.

A Rewrite these sentences in the passive. Then compare with a partner.

1 People are reusing more items every day. ______________________
2 People need to maintain cars for safety. ______________________
3 Guests are conserving water in hotels. ______________________
4 You have to discard old batteries properly. ______________________
5 Homeowners need to store chemicals safely. ______________________

B Complete the sentences with the present continuous passive or the infinitive passive. Then compare with a partner.

The Billabong clothing company has found an unusual way to make clothes. Plastic soda bottles and discarded clothing ______________ (combine) to make "eco-friendly" shorts. The company says that with this new material, environmental pollution ______________ (limit). For example, ten recycled bottles have ______________ (use) to make one pair of Billabong shorts; that means ten fewer bottles in landfills. Currently, the shorts ______________ (sell) for about $50.

4 Speaking Environmental trends

A Which trends are happening in your town, city, or country? Check (✓) your answers.

- ☐ More products are being reused.
- ☐ More water is being conserved.
- ☐ The air is becoming less polluted.
- ☐ More hybrid cars are being purchased.
- ☐ Money is being spent on "green" technology.
- ☐ More solar energy is being produced.

B GROUP WORK **Compare your answers. What do you think is causing each trend? Choose one trend that is not happening. What do you think needs to be done about it?**

5 Keep talking!

Go to page 149 for more practice.

I can discuss environmental trends.

B That's a good point.

1 Interactions Opinions

A **Do you do any of these activities when you travel? How could these activities affect the environment?**

bicycling	camping	hiking	kayaking	snorkeling	viewing wildlife

B **Listen to the conversation. Where does Daniela want to stay on vacation? Then practice the conversation.**

Elena Where are you going on vacation?

Daniela Maybe to this eco-friendly resort.

Elena What do you mean, "eco-friendly"?

Daniela Well, it combines eco-tourism and helping the local community. It's important to be responsible when you travel, don't you think?

Elena That's a good point.

Daniela So, this place looks good. They're trying to conserve water. And they want you to purchase handmade objects from the local businesses.

Elena Do you know who owns it?

Daniela I have no idea. Why do you ask?

Elena Well, some eco-resorts are owned by big companies, so the money they make doesn't help the local community very much.

Daniela I don't see it that way. Eco-resorts give jobs to local people and help raise environmental awareness, no matter who owns them.

C **Read the expressions below. Complete each box with a similar expression from the conversation. Then listen and check your answers.**

Supporting an opinion	Not supporting an opinion
______________________	______________________
I see what you mean.	I see it a little differently.
You make a very good point.	Actually, I have a different opinion.

D PAIR WORK **Share your opinions about eco-tourism Use the ideas below or your own idea. Support or don't support one another's opinions.**

builds environmental awareness	helps locals more than it hurts them
can actually damage the environment	is only a trendy marketing word

2 Listening A case for tap water?

A **Listen to the conversation between Eric and Mandy about bottled water. Number the pictures from 1 to 4.**

B **Listen again. Complete the sentences with the correct numbers.**

1 People in the U.S. spend more than ________ billion dollars a year on bottled water.
2 More than ________ % of bottled water is just tap water.
3 People are drinking ________ % more bottled water every year.
4 Manufacturing bottles uses ________ times the amount of water in the bottle.
5 The energy used to make plastic bottles can drive ________ million cars a year.
6 People in the U.S. buy ________ billion bottles of water a year.
7 Only ________ % of the bottles are being recycled.
8 It only costs ________ cents a gallon to get tap water in your home.

C **PAIR WORK** **Does Eric approve of buying bottled water? How do you feel about buying bottled water?**

3 Speaking Seeing both sides

GROUP WORK **Check (✓) the opinions you agree with. Then compare and discuss your opinions.**

- ☐ Schools should be required to serve only healthy food.
- ☐ Kids at school should be free to eat whatever food they want.
- ☐ Rich countries have to pay more to fight climate change.
- ☐ Every country has to pay more to fight climate change.
- ☐ The worst kind of pollution is air pollution.
- ☐ The worst kind of pollution is water pollution.
- ☐ The worst kind of pollution is land pollution.

A: *I think the worst kind of pollution is air pollution. If the air is dirty, people can't breathe.*

B: *I see it a little differently. Water pollution is worse because . . .*

I can take time to think in an interview.

C My community

1 Vocabulary Community improvement

A Complete the sentences. Then listen and check your answers.

1 A **beautiful project** makes a community ______.
   a. more attractive   b. less attractive
2 At a **community garden**, people ______.
   a. can go camping   b. grow vegetables or flowers
3 At an **employment center**, people can get ______.
   a. job information   b. marriage advice
4 At a **health clinic**, people can get medical ______.
   a. problems   b. help
5 With a **neighborhood watch**, neighbors try to limit ______.
   a. crime   b. pollution
6 A **public library** is used by ______.
   a. members only   b. everyone
7 A **recreation center** is a place to ______.
   a. help build homes   b. play sports or games
8 A **recycling center** is a place to ______.
   a. take used materials   b. get housing advice

B PAIR WORK Which services in Part A do you have in your community? What other services do you have in your community? Who do these services help?

A: I know we have a public library, a health clinic, and a recreation center.
B: But I don't think there's a community garden.

2 Conversation A better place to live

A Listen to the conversation. Who will a recreation center help?

Interviewer Hi. I'm with the community improvement board.
Mr. Brown Great. You guys are doing a fantastic job.
Interviewer Thank you. As you know, we no longer have a community garden because of a lack of interest. Would you want to build a recreation center instead?
Mr. Brown That's a good idea. We should build one so teens have a place to go.
Interviewer OK. Now, although we have a neighborhood watch, there's still crime. So we're planning on putting video cameras on streetlights –
Mr. Brown Great. There goes our privacy.
Interviewer So you won't support these cameras?

B Listen to the rest of the conversation. Which community improvement would Mr. Brown support? Which one wouldn't he support?

3 Grammar Linking words

Reason:	We no longer have a community garden **because of** a lack of interest.
Result:	There's still crime, **so** we're planning to install video cameras.
Contrast:	**Although** we have a neighborhood watch, there's still crime.
Condition:	Teens will have a place to go **if** we build a recreation center.
Purpose:	We should build a recreation center **so (that)** teens have a place to go.

A Circle the correct words. Then compare with a partner.

1 The city stopped all beautification projects **because of** / **so that** a lack of money.
2 Why don't you visit the employment center **if** / **so that** you need a job?
3 Let's go to the public library **because of** / **so that** we can borrow some books.
4 I'm not feeling well, **although** / **so** I'm going to go to the health clinic.
5 **Although** / **So** we have a community garden, few people know about it.
6 Crime in our community is down **because of** / **so that** the neighborhood watch.

B PAIR WORK Complete these sentences with your own ideas.

Although our town is safe, . . .	If you want a place to relax, . . .
I have a bag of empty cans, so . . .	We need to make changes because of . . .

4 Pronunciation Rise-falling and low falling tones

Listen and repeat. Notice the rise-falling and low falling tones in the responses. A rise-falling tone means you really mean what you're saying. A low falling tone can mean that you don't mean what you're saying.

A I'm with the community board. B Great. You guys are doing a fantastic job.

A We're putting in video cameras. B Great. There goes our privacy.

5 Speaking Quality of life

GROUP WORK How can you improve the quality of life for these people in your community? Share your ideas.

children	families	teenagers
the elderly	new arrivals	unemployed people

"Although there's playground equipment in the park, it's old. So I think we should raise money for new equipment."

6 Keep talking!

Go to page 150 for more practice.

I can discuss ways to improve my community.

D Getting involved

1 Reading

A What are some of the challenges young people face today?

B Read the article. According to Dr. Abreu, how can orchestra training help with the problems that children in poor neighborhoods face?

04/10/18

El Sistema: Social Change Through Music

In 1975, Dr. José Abreu, a musician and economist, wanted to do something about the poverty, violence, and hopelessness that many children experienced in his home nation of Venezuela. So he started an orchestra training program for children, known today as El Sistema.

It was not an obvious solution. At the time, there were just two orchestras in the entire country, and a classical music audience of only about 1,000. But Abreu believed that daily music instruction after school in a safe place would help protect children from violence on the streets. He thought that playing and learning together as a group could give children a sense of community and help them to learn to live in harmony with others. As Abreu says, "The orchestra is the only group that comes together with the sole purpose of agreement."

El Sistema is very different than most music programs. In traditional music education, a student might have one lesson each week for 30 minutes. In El Sistema, students study three to four hours every day. El Sistema students play and study in groups, rather than practicing alone.

Every learner is expected to be a teacher—once students have mastered a skill, it is their responsibility and privilege to teach it to another student. And while many music programs are available only to the best musicians, El Sistema is free and open to any child who wants to participate and work hard to improve.

The impact of this program is remarkable. Venezuela today has hundreds of orchestras for children, youth, and adults, and hundreds of thousands of children are being given daily music education. El Sistema has spread to 60 countries throughout the world. Although most who participate in El Sistema will not become professional musicians, the program is helping countless children gain a sense of accomplishment, develop strong social connections, and build creative and leadership skills.

C Read the article again. Answer the questions.

1 Why did Dr. Abreu start El Sistema? ______

2 What does playing music together help children to do? ______

3 How much time do students study each day? ______

4 Who may join an El Sistema program? ______

5 What skills is El Sistema helping to build? ______

D PAIR WORK How might this program change the adults and children who participate in it? Discuss your ideas.

2 Writing A letter to a community leader

A **Write a letter to a community leader about an issue that you feel needs to be addressed. Use these questions and the model to help you.**

- Who are you?
- What is the issue?
- What is currently being done?
- What needs to be done?

B **PAIR WORK** **Exchange letters with a partner. Do you agree?**

Dear Councilman Perez,

I am a third-year student at Union University. I am writing to express my concern about how difficult it is for people in wheelchairs to enter many buildings on campus. Although some public buildings have wheelchair ramps, most do not. The city needs to require that all buildings have ramps. . . .

3 Listening Helping out

A **Listen to three people talk about issues. Check (✓) the issue they're involved in.**

	Issue	What they're doing to help
Fernando *Fortaleza, Brazil*	☐ translating ☐ job training	
Aicha *Casablanca, Morocco*	☐ beautification projects ☐ parking issues	
Ingrid *Düsseldorf, Germany*	☐ helping new arrivals ☐ recreation centers	

B **Listen again. What are they doing to help? Write one example in the chart.**

C **Which issue in Part A are you concerned about? What other ways can people help?**

4 Speaking Raising awareness

A **Work with a partner. Agree on a charity, a cause, or an organization you would like people to be aware of. Then plan a way to raise awareness of the problem or its solution. Consider these ideas and ideas of your own.**

- organize a community event
- create a social networking group
- give presentations at schools
- have a contest to raise money
- pass out information on the street
- put up informational posters around town
- run public-service announcements on the radio
- set up an information table on the sidewalk
- set up an email marketing campaign

B **CLASS ACTIVITY** **Share your ideas with the class. Ask and answer questions for more information.**

I can discuss ways to raise awareness.

Wrap-up

1 Quick pair review

Lesson A Do you remember?

Match the active and passive sentences. You have one minute.

1 You need to limit your use of running water. ____
2 Our building is limiting our use of running water. ____
3 The office store is discarding printer ink. ____
4 You need to discard your printer ink at an office store. ____
5 You have to purchase "green" items online. ____

a. Your printer ink needs to be discarded at an office store.
b. Our use of running water is being limited.
c. "Green" items have to be purchased online.
d. Printer ink is being discarded by the office store.
e. Your use of running water needs to be limited.

Lesson B Give your opinion!

What do you think about these eco-friendly activities? Use expressions to support or not support your partner's opinion. You and your partner have two minutes.

Avoid using plastic bags.	Don't purchase a new cell phone every year.
Buy energy saving lightbulbs.	Take your own bags to a store.
Don't dump paint.	Walk to work.

A: *Don't dump paint.*
B: *That's a good point. Recycle it. For example, give it to a friend to use.*

Lesson C Brainstorm!

Make a list of community improvement ideas. How many can you remember? You have two minutes.

Lesson D Find out!

Who are two people that both you and your partner think are role models? You and your partner have two minutes.

2 In the real world

What is a problem in your community? Go online and find information about one of these problems, or choose your own idea. Find out about possible solutions. Then write about it.

- parking
- pollution
- traffic
- trash

Trash

People dump trash everywhere. There aren't enough trash cans for people to throw things away in. Trash cans need to be put on every corner in every city.

Keep talking!

News survey

A PAIR WORK **Interview your partner. Check (✓) his or her answers.**

ARE YOU A NEWS LOVER?

Do you always like to be up-to-date on the latest news? Are you a news lover? Complete this survey and find out.

1 Do you share interesting news stories with friends or family?

☐ yes ☐ no

2 Did you read or listen to a news story yesterday?

☐ yes ☐ no

3 Have you read or listened to a news story today?

☐ yes ☐ no

4 What area of news are you interested in? You can check (✓) as many as you want.

☐ world news ☐ national news ☐ local news

5 What types of news are you interested in? You can check (✓) as many as you want.

☐ business ☐ entertainment ☐ travel
☐ technology ☐ sports ☐ lifestyle
☐ health ☐ weather ☐ other: ____________

6 Where do you get your news? You can check (✓) as many as you want.

☐ newspapers ☐ radio ☐ the Internet
☐ magazines ☐ TV ☐ other: ____________

7 How much time do you spend learning about the news every day?

☐ 0–5 minutes ☐ 6–15 minutes ☐ 16 minutes or more

B PAIR WORK **Score your partner's answers. Add up his or her points to find the results.**

Questions 1–3	Questions 4–6	Question 7
no = 0 points	each ✓ = 2 points	0–5 minutes = 0 points
yes = 2 points		6–15 minutes = 4 points
		16+ minutes = 8 points

More than 20 points
You're definitely a news lover. You always want to know what's happening in the news.

11–19 points
You're a well-informed person. You balance your interest in the news with other interests.

0–10 points
You don't follow the news every day. You may not know what's going on in the world.

C GROUP WORK **Share the results. Do the results in Part B describe you well? What do you think the results say about your personality and interests?**

What's the question?

A Read the sentences. Write a *Wh-* or *yes / no* question.

1 He likes to be outdoors when the weather is nice.

2 I'm planning my next outdoor adventure.

3 We made a small fire when it got dark.

4 They were walking down the street when they heard a loud car crash.

5 He's seen snakes on a hiking trail.

6 I'll go camping next weekend.

B PAIR WORK **Compare your questions. How many of your questions are the same? What other questions can you make?**

C PAIR WORK **Write three sentences using words from the box and your own ideas. Then read the sentences to your partner. How many *Wh-* or *yes / no* questions can your partner make?**

attack	camping	crash	miss	rescue
bear	car	experiences	mountain	survive
boat	chase	fire	news	

1 Sentence:

2 Sentence:

3 Sentence:

Finding out more

A **Add two more topics to the chart.**

Find someone who's been . . . lately.	Name	Extra information
listening to songs in English		
saving money to buy something		
skipping breakfast		
planning a vacation		
spending a lot of time at the mall		
studying for an important exam		
getting up early		
chatting online in English		
playing sports on the weekend		
watching online videos		

B CLASS ACTIVITY **Find classmates who have been doing the things in Part A. Write their names and ask questions for more information. Write the extra information.**

A: *José, have you been listening to songs in English lately?*

B: *Yes, I have.*

A: *Really? What kinds of music have you been listening to?*

C CLASS ACTIVITY **Share the most interesting information.**

Communication with body language

A **Match each common North American gesture with its meaning.**

Be quiet.	Come here.	Hello.	Stop.	What time is it?
Call me.	Go ahead.	Speak louder.	Wait a moment.	

1 ____________ 4 ____________ 7 ____________

2 ____________ 5 ____________ 8 ____________

3 ____________ 6 ____________ 9 ____________

B GROUP WORK Act out a gesture from Part A. Your classmates guess what you're doing. Use these words when guessing.

ask	have	help	invite	let	make	remind	tell

A: *You're asking someone to stop.*

B: *Actually, I think you're making someone stop.*

C GROUP WORK What other gestures do you know? Act them out. Your classmates guess what you're doing.

Festival food

A PAIR WORK **Look at these popular festival foods. Which do you want to try? Which would you not want to try? Why? Tell your partner.**

Shaved ice
Ice is first shaved, and then a choice of different fruit syrups is added.

Elephant ear
Dough is pressed flat, fried in a pan, and then covered with sugar and cinnamon.

Turkey leg
A turkey leg is covered with sugar, salt, and spices and then roasted slowly.

Meatballs on a stick
Meatballs are baked, put on a stick, and then covered with tomato sauce.

Corn on the cob
An ear of corn is roasted and buttered. Salt, pepper, or hot sauce is then added.

Fried candy bar
A whole chocolate candy bar is covered in batter and then fried. Whipped cream is sometimes added on top.

B PAIR WORK **Close your books. Take turns. Describe one of the festival foods. Your partner guesses the food.**

C GROUP WORK **Discuss these questions.**

- Which foods in Part A are healthy? Which aren't? In what way?
- Which foods and drinks are popular at festivals in your country?
- How are they made? Who usually eats them?
- Are these foods different from street foods? If so, how?
- How does food vary in your country from region to region?
- Think about your hometown. Is it known for a particular food?

Fun food facts

A **PAIR WORK** **Interview your partner. Circle his or her answers. Do you agree?**

Secrets of the chefs

How many food tricks do you know? Try this quiz to find out.

1 Sometimes salt gets sticky in a salt shaker. What can you put in the salt shaker to fix the problem?

a. a coin b. rice c. tea leaves

2 What can you put on fruit as soon as you cut it so that it doesn't become brown?

a. milk b. sugar c. lemon juice

3 After you have used your microwave, what can you boil in it to clean it?

a. water and vinegar b. milk and butter c. coffee and sugar

4 Where can you put a green banana to make it become yellow?

a. in the fridge b. in the sun c. in a paper bag

5 When you put an egg into salty water, it floats. What does this mean?

a. It's fresh. b. It's not fresh. c. It's from a duck.

6 After you boil an egg, where can you put it so that you can peel it easily?

a. in cold water b. in salty water c. in the microwave

7 What can you put in a cookie jar to make cookies stay soft and chewy?

a. noodles b. sticky candy c. a piece of bread

8 Cutting onions makes people cry. What can you do to prevent this?

a. Chew gum. b. Add salt to them. c. Hold your breath.

B **PAIR WORK** **Check your guesses. How many food tricks did you know?**

1. b 2. c 3. a 4. c 5. b 6. a 7. c 8. a

Dilemmas

A **Read the questions. Circle your answers, or add your own ideas.**

1 What would you do if you found a lost pet in the street?

a. Tell someone.
b. Follow it.
c. Feed it.
d. Take it home.
e. Other: ________

2 What would you do if you accidentally hit a parked car?

a. Call the police.
b. Wait for the owner.
c. Leave a note.
d. Drive away.
e. Other: ________

3 What would you do if you found a cell phone on the subway?

a. Wait for someone to call.
b. Call the last number dialed.
c. Give it to a ticket agent.
d. Keep it.
e. Other: ________

4 What would you do if you didn't have money to pay for dinner?

a. Call someone.
b. Go to an ATM.
c. Let my friend pay.
d. Take it home.
e. Other: ________

5 What would you do if you saw someone take something from a store?

a. Talk to the person.
b. Tell the manager.
c. Call the police.
d. Look the other way.
e. Other: ________

6 What would you do if you accidentally broke a cup at your friend's?

a. Try to fix it.
b. Offer to pay for it.
c. Apologize.
d. Hide it.
e. Other: ________

B **GROUP WORK** **Discuss your answers. Do you agree?**

A: What would you do if you found a lost pet in the street?
B: I'd probably tell someone. What would you do?
C: I'd look for a name tag. If it didn't have one, I'd call the police.

Right and wrong

A **PAIR WORK** **Read the situations. Answer the questions. Discuss your answers.**

- Did the people do the right thing?
- If not, what should or shouldn't they have done?
- What could they have done differently?
- Would you have done anything differently? Why?

Jill and her husband Frank were flying to Thailand on vacation. The flight attendant offered one empty seat in business class to them. Because he's tall, Frank took the seat. Jill also wanted it, but Frank didn't ask her opinion. Now she's angry.

Steven invited Chuck and his wife Maria to his wedding. They accepted the invitation. Later Steven changed the wedding date, but Maria had a business trip then. So Chuck called Steven, offered an apology, and said they had to turn down his invitation. Steven was disappointed.

Tim borrowed his brother Mike's jacket without asking. Tim's girlfriend Allison accidentally spilled grape juice on the jacket. Mike saw the jacket the next day and asked for an explanation. Tim told the truth. Mike made Tim buy him a new jacket.

Lisa came home late and couldn't find her key. Her roommate Sue was sleeping. So Lisa broke a window to get inside. A neighbor heard the noise and called the police. Lisa offered a good explanation, and the police let her go. But Sue was very angry.

A: *I don't think that Frank did the right thing.*

B: *I agree. He shouldn't have moved up to business class. He could have . . .*

B **GROUP WORK** **Did any of your partner's answers surprise you? Do you and your partner agree on the people's behavior? Share your opinions.**

Travel adventure game

GROUP WORK **Work in a group of three. Play the game.**

Rules of the game

Student A: Choose a pair of pictures and compare them.
Student B: Make another comparison about the same pictures.
Student C: Make a different comparison about the same pictures.

A: *New York is more exciting than Miami.*

B: *Maybe, but Miami is more relaxing.*

C: *Miami is sunnier, too.*

Continue making comparisons. If someone can't make a comparison, he or she is "out."

The last person to make a comparison about the pair of pictures "wins."

The winner chooses a new pair of pictures, and the game begins with another comparison.

Cities

New York

Miami

Countries

Canada

Singapore

Transportation

train

plane

Places to stay

campground

youth hostel

Natural wonders

the Amazon rain forest

the Sahara desert

Landmarks

the Eiffel Tower

the Parthenon

What to do?

A **Imagine a friend has these travel problems. Write your advice.**

1 Your friend reserved a city tour online, but the tour guide can't find his reservation.

My advice: Buy a new ticket.
My partner's advice: ______

2 Your friend's checking in for his overseas flight, but he finds out his passport is expired.

My advice: ______
My partner's advice: ______

3 Your friend's been traveling all day, and he now finds out his hotel is overbooked.

My advice: ______
My partner's advice: ______

4 Your friend's train is going to be delayed an hour. He doesn't know why, and he's already late for an appointment.

My advice: ______
My partner's advice: ______

5 Your friend's been waiting at the baggage claim for his luggage, but his luggage is missing.

My advice: ______
My partner's advice: ______

6 Your friend expected nice weather for his beach vacation, but it's been raining for two days.

My advice: ______
My partner's advice: ______

B PAIR WORK **Interview your partner. Write your partner's advice.**

C GROUP WORK **Report your advice and your partner's advice. What are the advantages and disadvantages of each person's advice?**

A: I told my friend to buy a new ticket. Mario told him not to get upset.

B: I reminded him to show his reservation number. Christina advised him to talk to the owner.

The wishing game

GROUP WORK **Play the game. Put a small object on *Start*. Toss a coin.**

Move 1 space.

Heads

Move 2 spaces.

Tails

Read aloud the question and answer it. Then answer a follow-up question from each person in your group. If you land on *Ask your own question*, make up a question to ask someone else in your group.

A: "What do you wish you could spend less time doing?" I wish I could spend less time doing chores.

B: What is your least favorite chore?

START

Ask your own question.

Where do you wish you were right now?

FINISH

What do you wish you could spend less time doing?

What do you wish you could change about yourself?

Who do you wish you could spend more time with?

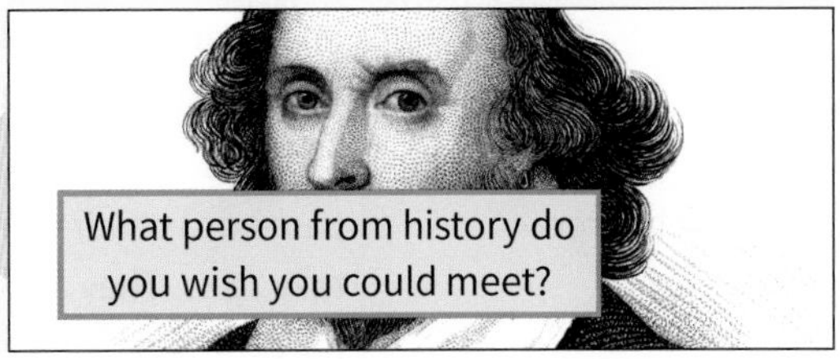

What do you wish you could do in class?

Ask your own question.

Which city do you wish you could visit?

Birth order and personality

A CLASS ACTIVITY **Find and write the names of two classmates who are:**

The first born (the oldest) in their family:

____________ ____________

The middle child:

____________ ____________

The last born (the youngest):

____________ ____________

An only child (no brothers or sisters):

____________ ____________

B **Read about your birth order. What does it show about your personality?**

Birth order	Personality	Careers	Fun fact
First-born children	First-born children are often ambitious, confident, logical, studious, and very organized.	First-born children are often people who become lawyers, doctors, and scientists.	Of the first 23 astronauts, 21were first-born children.
Middle-born children	Rebellious, competitive, independent, loyal, and imaginative are traits that often describe middle- born children.	Diplomats, artists, and designers are jobs that middle-born children are good at.	Middle-born children often make opposite decisions from first- borns.
Last-born children	Last-born children like to take risks. They are often hardworking, idealistic, outgoing, and very confident.	Firefighters, inventors, and actors are jobs that often attract last-born children.	Last-born children are often "the life of the party."
Only children	Only children are good problem-solvers. They're mature, responsible, energetic, and often very ambitious.	Similar to first-borns, only children are often lawyers, doctors, and scientists.	Elvis Presley, Indira Gandhi, and Frank Sinatra were all only children.

C PAIR WORK **Talk to a classmate from Part A with the same birth order as you. What kind of person are you? Do you agree with your personality description? Do you think the other descriptions are accurate for people you know?**

A: I don't agree with the description. I'm the first born in my family, but I'm a person who likes to take risks.

B: Really? I agree with the description. I'm the kind of person who is very organized.

You've got to have this!

A **Read the ads below. Choose one. Make a list of reasons to buy the product. Use these ideas and your own ideas.**

Flying alarm clock
Can't get up in the morning? When this alarm clock goes off, it flies around the room. You have to get out of bed to turn it off.

Keyboard waffle maker
Say good-bye to boring old waffles. This waffle maker makes the tasty breakfast treat in the shape of computer keyboards.

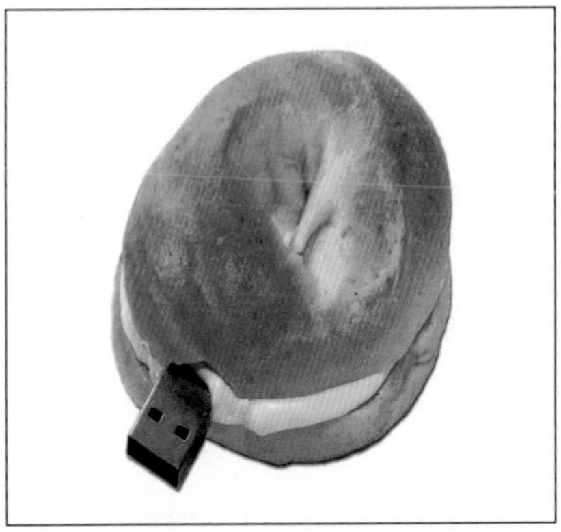

Bakery flash drives
Flash drives are such a great way to carry data. But why not make yours a little more interesting with these bakery items?

Gel ant house
Ants can be a little boring to watch – but not when they live in this world of green gel. When the ants move, the gel changes colors.

Mini motorcycle
Motorcycles have one wheel in front of the other, but this one has two side by side. Just turn it on, lean forward and go!

Umbrella light
No more walking home in the dark. This umbrella has a light inside. Just turn it on and you have a light – and a safe walk home.

B PAIR WORK **Take turns. Describe your product from Part A. Try to convince your partner to buy the product.**

"The umbrella light is such a convenient product that all of your friends will want one. You can keep it in your bag. It's so useful that you will never leave home without it."

C PAIR WORK **Would you buy your partner's product? Would you buy any of the products? Why or why not? Share your ideas.**

Product improvements

A PAIR WORK **Choose a product. What is it used for? What features does it have? Brainstorm all the things the product does.**

car	coffeemaker	hair dryer	refrigerator
cell phone	computer	headphones	TV

A: *A cell phone is used to call people.*

B: *They're used to check the time, text people, and . . .*

B PAIR WORK **Re-design your product. What words describe your product? What improvements have you made to your product? How is it used now?**

C GROUP WORK **Present your product to another pair.**

A: *We have developed a creative and useful product.*

B: *It is a flying car. It is terrific in traffic, and it will be very successful someday.*

Lucky Larry

A PAIR WORK Make a story. Number the pictures from 1 to 9.

Some people were moving a piano into the upstairs apartment, but they hadn't gotten it inside yet.

It took a long time to get home. Earlier, a police officer had stopped him for speeding.

He was very thankful that he hadn't been in the car at the time.

He went to the concert with Gail because she'd given him the tickets for his birthday.

He then realized he hadn't taken his umbrella from his apartment.

By the time he parked his car in front of his apartment, it had started to rain.

After he'd locked his car, he ran to the front door in the rain.

Larry drove home one evening. He'd been at a piano concert with his friend Gail.

He heard a very loud noise, so he turned around. The piano had fallen on his car!

B GROUP WORK Join another pair. Take turns. Tell your stories. Are they the same?

C GROUP WORK Close your books. Tell the story in your own words from memory.

A different path?

A **Read the topics in each box. Check (✓) three that were important moments in your life. Write an example of each and why these moments were important.**

"If I hadn't gone to summer camp, I wouldn't have met my best friend."

"I bought a new computer last summer, and now I can work from home."

Important moments in life	Examples and explanations
☐ a job you got ☐ a job you didn't get	
☐ someone you met who changed your life ☐ someone you wish you hadn't met	
☐ something you said to a friend ☐ something you didn't say to a friend	
☐ a place you visited ☐ a place you didn't visit	
☐ something you bought ☐ something you didn't buy	
☐ an exam you passed ☐ an exam you didn't pass	
☐ something you learned to do ☐ something you didn't learn to do	
☐ other: (your own idea)	

B GROUP WORK **Take turns. Talk about the important moments in your chart. Ask each other questions for more details. Then find out: How would things have been different without these moments?**

A: *One time, I missed my plane to Los Angeles.*

B: *Why were you going to Los Angeles?*

A: *I had an interview for an internship.*

C: *Why did you miss your plane?*

A: *I made a mistake and turned off my alarm. If I hadn't turned off the alarm, I wouldn't have missed my plane. I would have had the internship. And I would have gotten it, I'm sure.*

B: *Too bad.*

A logical explanation?

Students A and B

A PAIR WORK You have a picture of a home office AFTER something happened. What do you think might have happened? Think of as many explanations as you can.

B GROUP WORK Join classmates who have a BEFORE picture. Their picture shows the office five minutes before. Tell them what you think might have happened. Then find out what really happened.

A: *We think that someone might have . . .*

B: *Or someone could have . . .*

C: *Actually, here's what really happened . . .*

C PAIR WORK Now you have a BEFORE picture of a restaurant. Describe the scene. What has happened? What's happening?

D GROUP WORK Join classmates who have an AFTER picture. Their picture shows the restaurant five minutes after your picture. Listen to their ideas about what might have happened. Then tell them what really happened.

A logical explanation?

Students C and D

A PAIR WORK You have a BEFORE picture of a home office. Describe the scene. What has happened? What is happening?

B GROUP WORK Join classmates who have an AFTER picture. Their picture shows the office five minutes after your picture. Listen to their ideas about what might have happened. Then tell them what really happened.

A: *We think that someone might have . . .*

B: *Or someone could have . . .*

C: *Actually, here's what really happened . . .*

C PAIR WORK Now you have a picture of a restaurant AFTER something has happened. What do you think might have happened? Think of as many explanations as you can.

D GROUP WORK Join classmates who have a BEFORE picture. Their picture shows the restaurant five minutes before. Tell them what you think might have happened. Then find out what really happened.

Unsolved mysteries

A **GROUP WORK** **Choose a different picture from others in your group. Read about the picture. How can you explain the unsolved mystery? Take turns. Describe the mystery and answer the questions.**

A: *There is a manuscript that no one can read.*

B: *Do you know where it's from?*

A: *Yes, it's from Italy, but the manuscript isn't in Italian.*

C: *Do you have any idea if . . . ?*

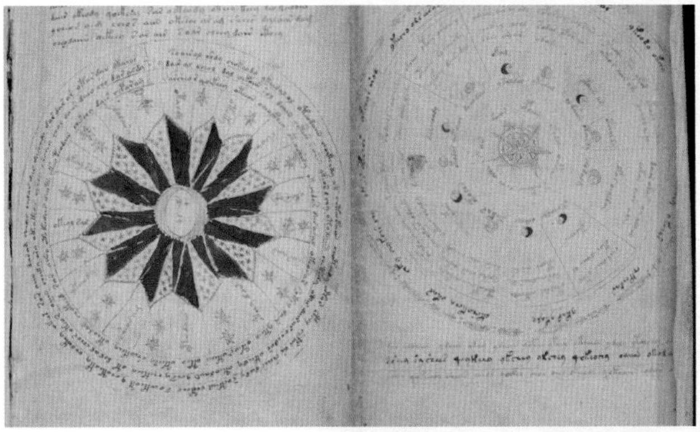

The Voynich manuscript is a book that was written in the 15th or 16th century. The author and alphabet are unknown. The book was discovered in Italy, but the language isn't like any European language. Even modern computers haven't "cracked" the code. Who wrote it, and why?

The Nazca lines are hundreds of "pictures" that were created in the Nazca Desert of Peru. They include birds, fish, spiders, monkeys, llamas, and lizards. How were they made? And why would anyone create such complicated pictures that you can only see from the air?

In the 1930s, workers in the Costa Rican jungle discovered mysterious stone balls that were perfectly round. Some were as small as a tennis ball, but others were larger – very large! They are human-made, but who made them, and how? What were they used for?

In 1947, something crashed near Roswell, New Mexico. At first the U.S. military said it was a "flying disc," but later changed its story and said it was a secret weather balloon. Others believe it was an alien spaceship. They think the government is hiding the truth. What crashed at Roswell?

B **CLASS ACTIVITY** **Describe other unexplained mysteries that you know about. Answer your classmates' questions.**

Find the differences

Student A

A PAIR WORK **You and your partner have a picture of the same accident. Tell your partner what the witnesses said in your picture. Your partner will report what other witnesses said. Find four differences in their reports.**

A: Peter told the police officer that the driver hadn't stopped at the light.

B: Jan also said he hadn't stopped at the light. She said that she'd seen the light turn yellow.

A: But Peter told the police officer he'd seen the light turn red. So that's different.

B PAIR WORK **Who do you think are the most reliable witnesses? The least reliable? Why? Whose fault was it – the driver's, the bicyclist's, or both? Why?**

Who said what?

A **Write a *yes* / *no* question for each topic.**

Topics	Questions	Notes: Who said what?
Work or school		
Entertainment		
Relationships		
Sports		
Past experiences		
Future goals		
other: (your own idea)		

B CLASS ACTIVITY **Ask different classmates your questions. Write their names. Take notes on the most interesting answers.**

A: *Claudia, have you ever arrived to college late?*

B: *I have. I arrived an hour late once because there was an accident on the highway.*

C GROUP WORK **Report your most interesting questions and answers.**

"I asked Claudia if she'd ever arrived to college late. She told me that she had . . ."

Find the differences

Student B

A PAIR WORK **You and your partner have a picture of the same accident. Tell your partner what the witnesses said in your picture. Your partner will report what other witnesses said. Find four differences in their reports.**

A: Peter told the police officer that the driver hadn't stopped at the light.

B: Jan also said he hadn't stopped at the light. She said that she'd seen the light turn yellow.

A: But Peter told the police officer he'd seen the light turn red. So that's different.

B PAIR WORK **Who do you think are the most reliable witnesses? The least reliable? Why? Whose fault was it – the driver's, the bicyclist's, or both? Why?**

Convenient services

A PAIR WORK **Look at the picture of the shopping mall. Where can you have or get these things done?**

get a doctor's prescription filled	have a résumé photocopied
get a passport photo taken	have a skirt made
get photos printed	have a suit cleaned
get your hair cut	have a watch repaired
get your nails done	have your eyes checked
have a computer virus removed	have your glasses fixed

A: You can get a passport photo taken at Picture It.

B: And maybe at Office Works.

B PAIR WORK **What else can you get or have done at the places in the picture? Tell your partner.**

C PAIR WORK **Where do you get or have things done near you? Use the ideas in Part A and ideas of your own.**

"I get my hair cut at Hair and Now. It's on Main Street, near my house."

Will that really happen?

A **Add three more question topics to the chart about life in the future.**

Find someone who believes . . . in the future.	Name
students will be finishing college in just three years	
most people will be eating only organic food	
women will be leading most countries in the world	
ocean levels will rise to dangerous levels	
the world's population will reach 10 billion	
children will work independently in classrooms	
people will be working a 20-hour workweek	
most people will be working until age 70	
most people will be speaking English as a native language	

B CLASS ACTIVITY **Ask questions and find classmates who believe the possibilities in Part A will be happening in the future. Write their names. Ask questions for more information.**

A: *In your opinion, will students be finishing college in just three years in the future?*

B: *Yes, they will.*

A: *Why do you think that will happen?*

B: *College will be even more expensive, so students will try to finish college faster.*

C GROUP WORK **Share your opinions about the possibilities in the chart. Do you agree with your classmates?**

The environmental game

PAIR WORK **Play the game. Put a small object on Start. Toss a coin.**

Move 1 space.

Heads

Move 2 spaces.

Tails

Answer the question: "What is being done in the picture?" Use the pictures and the words.

If your answer describes something that helps the environment, move forward one square.

If your answer describes something that hurts the environment, say what needs to be done and stay on the square.

A: *Heads. Conserve. Water is being conserved. That helps the environment.*

B: *Tails. Waste. Energy is being wasted. That doesn't help the environment. The lights need to be turned off.*

Beautification project

A GROUP WORK **Plan a community improvement project. Decide together on a project, and complete the information.**

What you'll make more beautiful:

- ☐ a park ☐ a road ☐ a playground ☐ a wall
- ☐ a river ☐ a sidewalk ☐ a building ☐ other: ____________

What you'll do:

- ☐ paint ☐ clean up ☐ rebuild ☐ plant ☐ other: ____________

What you'll need:

- ☐ trash bags ☐ shovels ☐ brooms ☐ paint
- ☐ flowers / plants ☐ tree ☐ gloves ☐ other: ____________

How long it will take: ____________ **Who will benefit:** ____________

Who will do which jobs: ____________ **What else you'll need to decide:** ____________

A: I think the front of the school needs to be more beautiful.

B: I agree. It looks old, so maybe we could paint it and plant flowers.

C: And if everyone helps, it will be a real school community project.

D: That's a good idea, although we would need to get permission first.

B CLASS ACTIVITY **Share your ideas. Decide on one project. How could you work together to complete the project?**

Irregular verbs

Base form	Simple past	Past participle
be	was, were	been
become	became	become
begin	began	begun
bite	bit	bitten
break	broke	broken
bring	brought	brought
build	built	built
buy	bought	bought
catch	caught	caught
choose	chose	chosen
come	came	come
cost	cost	cost
cut	cut	cut
do	did	done
draw	drew	drawn
drink	drank	drunk
drive	drove	driven
eat	ate	eaten
fall	fell	fallen
feel	felt	felt
find	found	found
forget	forgot	forgotten
get	got	gotten
give	gave	given
go	went	gone
grow	grew	grown
hang	hung	hung
have	had	had
hear	heard	heard
hold	held	held
hurt	hurt	hurt
keep	kept	kept

Base form	Simple past	Past participle
know	knew	known
leave	left	left
lend	lent	lent
lose	lost	lost
make	made	made
meet	met	met
pay	paid	paid
put	put	put
read	read	read
ride	rode	ridden
run	ran	run
say	said	said
see	saw	seen
sell	sold	sold
send	sent	sent
show	showed	shown
sing	sang	sung
sit	sat	sat
sleep	slept	slept
speak	spoke	spoken
spend	spent	spent
stand	stood	stood
stick	stuck	stuck
swim	swam	swum
take	took	taken
teach	taught	taught
tell	told	told
think	thought	thought
wake	woke	woken
wear	wore	worn
win	won	won
write	wrote	written

Credits

The authors and publishers acknowledge the following sources of copyright material and are grateful for the permissions granted. While every effort has been made, it has not always been possible to identify the sources of all the material used, or to trace all copyright holders. If any omissions are brought to our notice, we will be happy to include the appropriate acknowledgements on reprinting and in the next update to the digital edition, as applicable.

Text

U9: Text adapted from sources https://www.wired.com/2009/03/ff-perfectmemory/ & https://www.theguardian.com/science/2017/feb/08/total-recall-the-people-who-never-forget. Reproduced with kind permissions of Jill Price; **U6:** The Nine Enneagram Type Descriptions are copyrighted by The Enneagram Institute and are used in the Four Corners Second Edition SB4 with permission; **U12:** Text adapted from reproduced "The Fundamentals of El Sistema". Copyright © 2017. Reproduced with the kind permission of Eric Booth.

Photography

All below images are sourced from Getty Images.

U1: ©Image Source/Getty Images; kizilkayaphotos/iStock/Getty Images Plus; ChamilleWhite/iStock/Getty Images Plus; fotog; Monty Rakusen/Cultura; ©Buena Vista Images/Getty images; ©White Packert/Getty Images; Ramn Carretero/EyeEm; JUSTIN TALLIS/AFP; Johannes Kroemer/The Image Bank; burwellphotography/E+; **U2:** Steve Debenport/E+; Hero Images; Hero Creative/Cultura; Betsie Van Der Meer/Taxi; Azemdega/E+; Lane Oatey/Blue Jean Images; mediaphotos/iStock/Getty Images Plus; vgajic/E+; AntonioGuillem/iStock/Getty Images Plus; PeopleImages/E+; Topic Images Inc.; Wavebreakmedia/iStock/Getty Images Plus; Roy Hsu/Blend Images; SSPL/Hulton Archive; **U3:** Dennis Gttlieb; Marik Lengauer/EyeEm; Tetra Images; gerenme/iStock/Getty Images Plus; lucentius/iStock/Getty Images Plus; nycshooter/iStock/Getty Images Plus; STILLFX/iStock/Getty Images Plus; desertsolitaire/iStock/Getty Images Plus; ©Danita Delimont/Getty Images; DebbiSmirnoff/iStock/Getty Images Plus; Foodcollection RF; Alter_photo/iStock/Getty Images Plus; PeterHermesFurian/iStock/Getty Images Plus; William Reavell/Dorling Kindersley; Barcin/E+; GEOFF KIDD/Science Photo Library/Getty Images Plus; Maksym Narodenko/iStock/Getty Images Plus; margouillatphotos/iStock/Getty Images Plus; WesAbrams/iStock/Getty Images Plus; James A. Guilliam/Photolibrary; deepblue4you/iStock/Getty Images Plus; Andy Crawford/Dorling Kindersley; Juanmonino/E+;Dorling Kindersley;Hemera Technologies/PhotoObjects.net/Getty Images Plus; Belyaevskiy/iStock/Getty Images Plus; Philip Wilkins/Photolibrary; Natikka/iStock/Getty Images Plus; 23d7d4d_101/iStock/Getty Images Plus; OLEKSANDR PEREPELYTSIA/iStock/Getty Images Plus; NJPhotos/iStock/Getty Images Plus; Peter Muller/Cultura; Tobias Titz; Jessica Boone/The Image Bank; 5second/iStock/Getty Images Plus; Nicola Tree/DigitalVision; Pinghung Chen/EyeEm; **U4:** VladimirFLoyd/iStock/Getty Images Plus; Eric Audras/ONOKY; **U5:** Tuul & Bruno Morandi/The Image Bank; gertvansanten/iStock Editorial/Getty Images Plus; diegograndi/iStock/Getty Images Plus; KeongDaGreat/iStock/Getty Images Plus; Edwin Remsberg/Photolibrary; tupungato/iStock Editorial/Getty Images Plus; ©Matt Cardy/Getty Images; **U6:** ©Brian Leatart/Getty Images; Image Source; Kritchanut/iStock/Getty Images Plus; Jupiterimages/The Image Bank; Alexis Paige/iStock/Getty Images Plus; Peter Dazeley/Photographer's Choice; altrendo images/Juice Images; pagadesign/iStock/Getty Images Plus; Lena Clara; ©Frank Siteman – Rainbow/Getty Images; Don Mason/Blend Images; **U7:** ©Original from Gwoeii/Getty images; RunPhoto/DigitalVision; Manakin/iStock Editorial/Getty Images Plus; sborisov/iStock/Getty Images Plus; kapulya/iStock/Getty Images Plus; sborisov/iStock/Getty Images Plus; kapulya/iStock/Getty Images Plus; fotomirc/iStock/Getty Images Plus; Dave King/Dorling Kindersley; LivingImages/iStock/Getty Images Plus; Museum of Science and Industry, Chicago/Archive Photos; ThomasVogel/iStock/Getty Images Plus; ivan-96/iStock/Getty Images Plus; Maxiphoto/iStock Editorial/Getty Images Plus; **U8:** Pekic/E+; Maskot; WALTER ZERLA/Cultura; South_agency/iStock/Getty Images Plus; fizkes/iStock/Getty Images Plus; Hybrid Images/Cultura; Georgethefourth/iStock/Getty Images Plus; MachineHeadz/iStock/Getty Images Plus; Giantstep Inc/Photodisc; PeopleImages/E+; Cultura RM Exclusive/Robin James; dimarik/iStock/Getty Images Plus; Jon Furniss/Wireimage; **U9:** altrendo images/Juice Images; Radius Images; ElleFitz/iStock/Getty Images Plus; lolostock/iStock/Getty Images Plus; Zoonar RF/Getty Images Plus; Bettmann; Dan Tuffs/Getty Images News; **U10:** siur/iStock/Getty Images Plus; paul mansfield photography/Moment; Nine OK/Photographer's Choice; paul mansfield photography/Moment; Paul Mansfield; ; ©Chris Whitehead/Getty images; MARTIN BUREAU/AFP; Ghislain & Marie David de Lossy/The Image Bank; Jon Kopaloff/FilmMagic; **U11:** braverabbit/iStock/Getty Images Plus; Eco/Universal Images Group; YakobchukOlena/iStock/Getty Images Plus; cyano66/iStock/Getty Images Plus; Kim Steele/Photodisc; warrengoldswain/iStock/Getty Images Plus; BJI/Blue Jean Images; NicoElNino/iStock/Getty Images Plus; Giulio_Fornasar/iStock/Getty Images Plus; ©Stephen Derr/Getty images; Lisa-Blue/iStock/Getty Images Plus; Dave and Les Jacobs/Lloyd Dobbie/Blend Images; ; Hero Images; aluxum/E+; Hero Images; isitsharp/iStock/Getty Images Plus; Viaframe/Corbis; **U12:** Maik Mitschke/EyeEm; Toa55/iStock/Getty Images Plus; ©Spencer Platt/Getty images; John Seaton Callahan/Moment; Frederic Cirou/PhotoAlto Agency RF Collections; Tetra Images; Photick/Sigrid Olsson/Getty Images Plus; bariskaradeniz/iStock/Getty Images Plus; asiseeit/E+; Blend Images - KidStock/Brand X Pictures; JackF/iStock/Getty Images Plus; bbostjan/iStock/Getty Images Plus; ; JUAN BARRETO/AFP; Simon Jarratt/Corbis/VCG/Getty Images; **End Matter:** Steven Cannon/EyeEm; SchulteProductions/iStock/Getty Images Plus; SafakOguz/iStock/Getty Images Plus; Hill Street Studios/Blend Images; gchapel/iStock/Getty Images Plus; bhofack2/iStock/Getty Images Plus; Daxus/iStock/Getty Images Plus; popksr/iStock/Getty Images Plus; grandriver/iStock/Getty Images Plus; bhofack2/iStock/Getty Images Plus; Sebalos/iStock/Getty Images Plus; Foodcollection RF; Qwart/iStock/Getty Images Plus; Rermrat Kaewpukdee/EyeEm; Goldfinch4ever/iStock/Getty Images Plus; ThamKC/iStock/Getty Images Plus; chikaphotograph/iStock/Getty Images Plus; liubovi samoilova/iStock/Getty Images Plus; Berna Namoglu/EyeEm; Jolanta Petraityte/EyeEm; Cebas/iStock/Getty Images Plus; Allan Baxter/The Image Bank; Scott B Smith

Photography/Photolibrary; RENAULT Philippe/hemis.fr; Carlina Teteris/Moment; Jeremy Horner/Corbis Documentary; Bloomberg/Getty Images; Helena Smith/Photolibrary; VisitBritain/Britain on View; Pedro Hélder da Costa Pinheiro/iStock/Getty Images Plus; ali suliman/iStock/Getty Images Plus; Cultura Exclusive/William Perugini; Jean-Pierre Lescourret/Lonely Planet Images; DoxaDigital/E+; furtaev/iStock/Getty Images Plus; Yiu Yu Hoi/DigitalVision; Chris Beall/Lonely Planet Images; David Zaitz/Photonica; izusek/E+; g-stockstudio/iStock/Getty Images Plus; g-stockstudio/iStock/Getty Images Plus; RuslanGuzov/iStock/Getty Images Plus; 81a/Photolibrary/Stockbyte/Getty Images Plus; sergey02/iStock/Getty Images Plus; Westend61; DoucetPh/iStock Editorial/Getty Images Plus; Studioofcrayons/iStock/Getty Images Plus; Image Source/Photodisc; marugod83/iStock/Getty Images Plus; Clerkenwell/Vetta; Monty Rakusen/Cultura; airdone/iStock/Getty Images Plus; Times/Getty Images.

Front cover by VisitBritain; Hero Images; Patchareeporn Sakoolchai/Moment.
Back cover by Monty Rakusen/Cultura.
The following images are sourced from other libraries:
U1: ©BAE/Alamy; ©David J. Green/Alamy; ©Age Fotostock; ©Craig Lovell/Alamy; ©Tetra Images/Alamy; ©Age Fotostock; ©Frank Veronsky; ©Insadco Photography/Alamy; ©NASA; © Twitter; ©Nick Ridley/Oxford Scientific/Getty Images; **U2:** ©Frank Veronsky; **U3:** ©Miguel Sobreira/Alamy; ©Newell Nussbaumer; ©Istock Photos; ©JG Photography/Alamy; ©Media Bakery; ©Mitch Diamond/Alamy; ©Media Bakery; ©Istock Photos; ©J Marshall/Tribaleye Images/Alamy; ©Frank Veronsky; **U4:** ©Frank Veronsky; **U5:** ©Frans Lemmens/Getty images; ©Media Bakery; Rob Schuster; **U6:** ©Media Bakery; ©Corbis/Alamy; ©Marmaduke St. John/Alamy; **U7:** ©Lukas Miglinas/Alamy; ©The Image Works; ©National Geographic; Andreblais/Dreamstime; Kyodo News/Newscom; Ed Bailey/AP Photo; **U8:** F.G.I CO., LTD./Alamy; **U9:** ©Frank Veronsky; **U10:** ©Kip Evans/Alamy; **U11:** ©Kip Evans/Alamy; **U12:** MAISANT Ludovic/hemis/Age Fotostock; ©Frank Veronsky; **End Matter:** © US mint; ©Courtesy of Think Geek; Messy Desk Design LLC; ©Bupkes Bakery; ©Ant Works; ©Motorcycle Mojo Magazine; ©Clever Care; Art Collection 2/Alamy; Carver Mostardi/Media Bakery; ©Manor Photography/Alamy.

Illustration
Front Matter: Kim Johnson; **U1:** ©Archangelo Entertainment/Kobal Collection; Kveta Jelinek; Dean MacAdam; QBS Learning; **U3:** Kim Johnson; **U4:** Dani Geremia/Beehive Illustration; QBS Learning; Kim Johnson; **U5:** QBS Learning; Kim Johnson; **U6:** QBS Learning; **U7:** QBS Learning; Kim Johnson; **U9:** Dani Geremia/Beehive Illustration; QBS Learning; Belgin Wedman; **U10–11:** QBS Learning; **End Matter:** Szilvia Szakall/Beehive Illustration; Dani Geremia/Beehive Illustration; Kim Johnson; QBS Learning.

Art direction, book design, and layout services: QBS Learning
Audio production: CityVox, NYC and John Marshall Media
Video production: Steadman Productions